Mometrix
TEST PREPARATION

I0866893

TerraNova® NEXT

Grade 4 Reading and Language Test Prep Guide

Written and edited by the Mometrix Test Preparation Team
Printed in the United States of America

Table of Contents

Introduction

Thank you for purchasing this resource! You have made the choice to prepare yourself for a test that could have a huge impact on your future, and this guide is designed to help you be fully ready for test day. Obviously, it's important to have a solid understanding of the test material, but you also need to be prepared for the unique environment and stressors of the test, so that you can perform to the best of your abilities.

For this purpose, the first section that appears in this guide is the **Success Strategies**. We've devoted countless hours to meticulously researching what works and what doesn't, and we've boiled down our findings to the most impactful steps you can take to improve your performance on the test. We start at the beginning with study planning and move through the preparation process, all the way to the testing strategies that will help you get the most out of what you know when you're finally sitting in front of the test.

We recommend that you start preparing for your test as far in advance as possible. However, if you've bought this guide as a last-minute study resource and only have a few days before your test, we recommend that you skip over the first two Success Strategies since they address a long-term study plan.

If you struggle with **test anxiety**, we strongly encourage you to check out our recommendations for how you can overcome it. Test anxiety is a formidable foe, but it can be beaten, and we want to make sure you have the tools you need to defeat it.

Strategy #1 – Plan Big, Study Small

There's a lot riding on your performance. If you want to ace this test, you're going to need to keep your skills sharp and the material fresh in your mind. You need a plan that lets you review everything you need to know while still fitting in your schedule. We'll break this strategy down into three categories.

Information Organization

Start with the information you already have: the official test outline. From this, you can make a complete list of all the concepts you need to cover before the test. Organize these concepts into groups that can be studied together, and create a list of any related vocabulary you need to learn so you can brush up on any difficult terms. You'll want to keep this vocabulary list handy once you actually start studying since you may need to add to it along the way.

Time Management

Once you have your set of study concepts, decide how to spread them out over the time you have left before the test. Break your study plan into small, clear goals so you have a manageable task for each day and know exactly what you're doing. Then just focus on one small step at a time. When you manage your time this way, you don't need to spend hours at a time studying. Studying a small block of content for a short period each day helps you retain information better and avoid stressing over how much you have left to do. You can relax knowing that you have a plan to cover everything in time. In order for this strategy to be effective though, you have to start studying early and stick to your schedule. Avoid the exhaustion and futility that comes from last-minute cramming!

Study Environment

The environment you study in has a big impact on your learning. Studying in a coffee shop, while probably more enjoyable, is not likely to be as fruitful as studying in a quiet room. It's important to keep distractions to a minimum. You're only planning to study for a short block of time, so make the most of it. Don't pause to check your phone or get up to find a snack. It's also important to **avoid multitasking**. Research has consistently shown that multitasking will make your studying dramatically less effective. Your study area should also be comfortable and well-lit so you don't have the distraction of straining your eyes or sitting on an uncomfortable chair.

The time of day you study is also important. You want to be rested and alert. Don't wait until just before bedtime. Study when you'll be most likely to comprehend and remember. Even better, if you know what time of day your test will be, set that time aside for study. That way your brain will be used to working on that subject at that specific time and you'll have a better chance of recalling information.

Finally, it can be helpful to team up with others who are studying for the same test. Your actual studying should be done in as isolated an environment as possible, but the work of organizing the information and setting up the study plan can be divided up. In between study sessions, you can discuss with your teammates the concepts that you're all studying and quiz each other on the details. Just be sure that your teammates are as serious about the test as you are. If you find that your study time is being replaced with social time, you might need to find a new team.

Strategy #2 – Make Your Studying Count

You're devoting a lot of time and effort to preparing for this test, so you want to be absolutely certain it will pay off. This means doing more than just reading the content and hoping you can remember it on test day. It's important to make every minute of study count. There are two main areas you can focus on to make your studying count.

Retention

It doesn't matter how much time you study if you can't remember the material. You need to make sure you are retaining the concepts. To check your retention of the information you're learning, try recalling it at later times with minimal prompting. Try carrying around flashcards and glance at one or two from time to time or ask a friend who's also studying for the test to quiz you.

To enhance your retention, look for ways to put the information into practice so that you can apply it rather than simply recalling it. If you're using the information in practical ways, it will be much easier to remember. Similarly, it helps to solidify a concept in your mind if you're not only reading it to yourself but also explaining it to someone else. Ask a friend to let you teach them about a concept you're a little shaky on (or speak aloud to an imaginary audience if necessary). As you try to summarize, define, give examples, and answer your friend's questions, you'll understand the concepts better and they will stay with you longer. Finally, step back for a big picture view and ask yourself how each piece of information fits with the whole subject. When you link the different concepts together and see them working together as a whole, it's easier to remember the individual components.

Finally, practice showing your work on any multi-step problems, even if you're just studying. Writing out each step you take to solve a problem will help solidify the process in your mind, and you'll be more likely to remember it during the test.

Modality

Modality simply refers to the means or method by which you study. Choosing a study modality that fits your own individual learning style is crucial. No two people learn best in exactly the same way, so it's important to know your strengths and use them to your advantage.

For example, if you learn best by visualization, focus on visualizing a concept in your mind and draw an image or a diagram. Try color-coding your notes, illustrating them, or creating symbols that will trigger your mind to recall a learned concept. If you learn best by hearing or discussing information, find a study partner who learns the same way or read aloud to yourself. Think about how to put the information in your own words. Imagine that you are giving a lecture on the topic and record yourself so you can listen to it later.

For any learning style, flashcards can be helpful. Organize the information so you can take advantage of spare moments to review. Underline key words or phrases. Use different colors for different categories. Mnemonic devices (such as creating a short list in which every item starts with the same letter) can also help with retention. Find what works best for you and use it to store the information in your mind most effectively and easily.

Strategy #3 – Practice the Right Way

Your success on test day depends not only on how many hours you put into preparing, but also on whether you prepared the right way. It's good to check along the way to see if your studying is paying off. One of the most effective ways to do this is by taking practice tests to evaluate your progress. Practice tests are useful because they show exactly where you need to improve. Every time you take a practice test, pay special attention to these three groups of questions:

- The questions you got wrong
- The questions you had to guess on, even if you guessed right
- The questions you found difficult or slow to work through

This will show you exactly what your weak areas are, and where you need to devote more study time. Ask yourself why each of these questions gave you trouble. Was it because you didn't understand the material? Was it because you didn't remember the vocabulary? Do you need more repetitions on this type of question to build speed and confidence? Dig into those questions and figure out how you can strengthen your weak areas as you go back to review the material.

Additionally, many practice tests have a section explaining the answer choices. It can be tempting to read the explanation and think that you now have a good understanding of the concept. However, an explanation likely only covers part of the question's broader context. Even if the explanation makes perfect sense, **go back and investigate** every concept related to the question until you're positive you have a thorough understanding.

As you go along, keep in mind that the practice test is just that: practice. Memorizing these questions and answers will not be very helpful on the actual test because it is unlikely to have any of the same exact questions. If you only know the right answers to the sample questions, you won't be prepared for the real thing. **Study the concepts** until you understand them fully, and then you'll be able to answer any question that shows up on the test.

It's important to wait on the practice tests until you're ready. If you take a test on your first day of study, you may be overwhelmed by the amount of material covered and how much you need to learn. Work up to it gradually.

On test day, you'll need to be prepared for answering questions, managing your time, and using the test-taking strategies you've learned. It's a lot to balance, like a mental marathon that will have a big impact on your future. Like training for a marathon, you'll need to start slowly and work your way up. When test day arrives, you'll be ready.

Start with the strategies you've read in the first two Success Strategies—plan your course and study in the way that works best for you. If you have time, consider using multiple study resources to get different approaches to the same concepts. It can be helpful to see difficult concepts from more than one angle. Then find a good source for practice tests. Many times, the test website will suggest potential study resources or provide sample tests.

Practice Test Strategy

If you're able to find at least three practice tests, we recommend this strategy:

Untimed and Open-Book Practice

Take the first test with no time constraints and with your notes and study guide handy. Take your time and focus on applying the strategies you've learned.

Timed and Open-Book Practice

Take the second practice test open-book as well, but set a timer and practice pacing yourself to finish in time.

Timed and Closed-Book Practice

Take any other practice tests as if it were test day. Set a timer and put away your study materials. Sit at a table or desk in a quiet room, imagine yourself at the testing center, and answer questions as quickly and accurately as possible.

Keep repeating timed and closed-book tests on a regular basis until you run out of practice tests or it's time for the actual test. Your mind will be ready for the schedule and stress of test day, and you'll be able to focus on recalling the material you've learned.

Strategy #4 – Pace Yourself

Once you're fully prepared for the material on the test, your biggest challenge on test day will be managing your time. Just knowing that the clock is ticking can make you panic even if you have plenty of time left. Work on pacing yourself so you can build confidence against the time constraints of the exam. Pacing is a difficult skill to master, especially in a high-pressure environment, so **practice is vital**.

Set time expectations for your pace based on how much time is available. For example, if a section has 60 questions and the time limit is 30 minutes, you know you have to average 30 seconds or less per question in order to answer them all. Although 30 seconds is the hard limit, set 25 seconds per question as your goal, so you reserve extra time to spend on harder questions. When you budget extra time for the harder questions, you no longer have any reason to stress when those questions take longer to answer.

Don't let this time expectation distract you from working through the test at a calm, steady pace, but keep it in mind so you don't spend too much time on any one question. Recognize that taking extra time on one question you don't understand may keep you from answering two that you do understand later in the test. If your time limit for a question is up and you're still not sure of the answer, mark it and move on, and come back to it later if the time and the test format allow. If the testing format doesn't allow you to return to earlier questions, just make an educated guess; then put it out of your mind and move on.

On the easier questions, be careful not to rush. It may seem wise to hurry through them so you have more time for the challenging ones, but it's not worth missing one if you know the concept and just didn't take the time to read the question fully. Work efficiently but make sure you understand the question and have looked at all of the answer choices, since more than one may seem right at first.

Even if you're paying attention to the time, you may find yourself a little behind at some point. You should speed up to get back on track, but do so wisely. Don't panic; just take a few seconds less on each question until you're caught up. Don't guess without thinking, but do look through the answer choices and eliminate any you know are wrong. If you can get down to two choices, it is often worthwhile to guess from those. Once you've chosen an answer, move on and don't dwell on any that you skipped or had to hurry through. If a question was taking too long, chances are it was one of the harder ones, so you weren't as likely to get it right anyway.

On the other hand, if you find yourself getting ahead of schedule, it may be beneficial to slow down a little. The more quickly you work, the more likely you are to make a careless mistake that will affect your score. You've budgeted time for each question, so don't be afraid to spend that time. Practice an efficient but careful pace to get the most out of the time you have.

Test-Taking Strategies

This section contains a list of test-taking strategies that you may find helpful as you work through the test. By taking what you know and applying logical thought, you can maximize your chances of answering any question correctly!

It is very important to realize that every question is different and every person is different: no single strategy will work on every question, and no single strategy will work for every person. That's why we've included all of them here, so you can try them out and determine which ones work best for different types of questions and which ones work best for you.

Question Strategies

⊘ Read Carefully

Read the question and the answer choices carefully. Don't miss the question because you misread the terms. You have plenty of time to read each question thoroughly and make sure you understand what is being asked. Yet a happy medium must be attained, so don't waste too much time. You must read carefully and efficiently.

⊘ Contextual Clues

Look for contextual clues. If the question includes a word you are not familiar with, look at the immediate context for some indication of what the word might mean. Contextual clues can often give you all the information you need to decipher the meaning of an unfamiliar word. Even if you can't determine the meaning, you may be able to narrow down the possibilities enough to make a solid guess at the answer to the question.

⊘ Prefixes

If you're having trouble with a word in the question or answer choices, try dissecting it. Take advantage of every clue that the word might include. Prefixes can be a huge help. Usually, they allow you to determine a basic meaning. *Pre-* means before, *post-* means after, *pro-* is positive, *de-* is negative. From prefixes, you can get an idea of the general meaning of the word and try to put it into context.

⊘ Hedge Words

Watch out for critical hedge words, such as *likely, may, can, often, almost, mostly, usually, generally, rarely,* and *sometimes.* Question writers insert these hedge phrases to cover every possibility. Often an answer choice will be wrong simply because it leaves no room for exception. Be on guard for answer choices that have definitive words such as *exactly* and *always.*

⊘ Switchback Words

Stay alert for *switchbacks.* These are the words and phrases frequently used to alert you to shifts in thought. The most common switchback words are *but, although,* and *however.* Others include *nevertheless, on the other hand, even though, while, in spite of, despite,* and *regardless of.* Switchback words are important to catch because they can change the direction of the question or an answer choice.

✓ FACE VALUE

When in doubt, use common sense. Accept the situation in the problem at face value. Don't read too much into it. These problems will not require you to make wild assumptions. If you have to go beyond creativity and warp time or space in order to have an answer choice fit the question, then you should move on and consider the other answer choices. These are normal problems rooted in reality. The applicable relationship or explanation may not be readily apparent, but it is there for you to figure out. Use your common sense to interpret anything that isn't clear.

Answer Choice Strategies

✓ ANSWER SELECTION

The most thorough way to pick an answer choice is to identify and eliminate wrong answers until only one is left, then confirm it is the correct answer. Sometimes an answer choice may immediately seem right, but be careful. The test writers will usually put more than one reasonable answer choice on each question, so take a second to read all of them and make sure that the other choices are not equally obvious. As long as you have time left, it is better to read every answer choice than to pick the first one that looks right without checking the others.

✓ ANSWER CHOICE FAMILIES

An answer choice family consists of two (in rare cases, three) answer choices that are very similar in construction and cannot all be true at the same time. If you see two answer choices that are direct opposites or parallels, one of them is usually the correct answer. For instance, if one answer choice says that quantity x increases and another either says that quantity x decreases (opposite) or says that quantity y increases (parallel), then those answer choices would fall into the same family. An answer choice that doesn't match the construction of the answer choice family is more likely to be incorrect. Most questions will not have answer choice families, but when they do appear, you should be prepared to recognize them.

✓ ELIMINATE ANSWERS

Eliminate answer choices as soon as you realize they are wrong, but make sure you consider all possibilities. If you are eliminating answer choices and realize that the last one you are left with is also wrong, don't panic. Start over and consider each choice again. There may be something you missed the first time that you will realize on the second pass.

✓ AVOID FACT TRAPS

Don't be distracted by an answer choice that is factually true but doesn't answer the question. You are looking for the choice that answers the question. Stay focused on what the question is asking for so you don't accidentally pick an answer that is true but incorrect. Always go back to the question and make sure the answer choice you've selected actually answers the question and is not merely a true statement.

✓ EXTREME STATEMENTS

In general, you should avoid answers that put forth extreme actions as standard practice or proclaim controversial ideas as established fact. An answer choice that states the "process should be used in certain situations, if..." is much more likely to be correct than one that states the "process should be discontinued completely." The first is a calm rational statement and doesn't even make a definitive, uncompromising stance, using a hedge word *if* to provide wiggle room, whereas the second choice is far more extreme.

⊘ Benchmark

As you read through the answer choices and you come across one that seems to answer the question well, mentally select that answer choice. This is not your final answer, but it's the one that will help you evaluate the other answer choices. The one that you selected is your benchmark or standard for judging each of the other answer choices. Every other answer choice must be compared to your benchmark. That choice is correct until proven otherwise by another answer choice beating it. If you find a better answer, then that one becomes your new benchmark. Once you've decided that no other choice answers the question as well as your benchmark, you have your final answer.

⊘ Predict the Answer

Before you even start looking at the answer choices, it is often best to try to predict the answer. When you come up with the answer on your own, it is easier to avoid distractions and traps because you will know exactly what to look for. The right answer choice is unlikely to be word-for-word what you came up with, but it should be a close match. Even if you are confident that you have the right answer, you should still take the time to read each option before moving on.

General Strategies

⊘ Tough Questions

If you are stumped on a problem or it appears too hard or too difficult, don't waste time. Move on! Remember though, if you can quickly check for obviously incorrect answer choices, your chances of guessing correctly are greatly improved. Before you completely give up, at least try to knock out a couple of possible answers. Eliminate what you can and then guess at the remaining answer choices before moving on.

⊘ Check Your Work

Since you will probably not know every term listed and the answer to every question, it is important that you get credit for the ones that you do know. Don't miss any questions through careless mistakes. If at all possible, try to take a second to look back over your answer selection and make sure you've selected the correct answer choice and haven't made a costly careless mistake (such as marking an answer choice that you didn't mean to mark). This quick double check should more than pay for itself in caught mistakes for the time it costs.

⊘ Pace Yourself

It's easy to be overwhelmed when you're looking at a page full of questions; your mind is confused and full of random thoughts, and the clock is ticking down faster than you would like. Calm down and maintain the pace that you have set for yourself. Especially as you get down to the last few minutes of the test, don't let the small numbers on the clock make you panic. As long as you are on track by monitoring your pace, you are guaranteed to have time for each question.

⊘ Don't Rush

It is very easy to make errors when you are in a hurry. Maintaining a fast pace in answering questions is pointless if it makes you miss questions that you would have gotten right otherwise. Test writers like to include distracting information and wrong answers that seem right. Taking a little extra time to avoid careless mistakes can make all the difference in your test score. Find a pace that allows you to be confident in the answers that you select.

✓ Keep Moving

Panicking will not help you pass the test, so do your best to stay calm and keep moving. Taking deep breaths and going through the answer elimination steps you practiced can help to break through a stress barrier and keep your pace.

Final Notes

The combination of a solid foundation of content knowledge and the confidence that comes from practicing your plan for applying that knowledge is the key to maximizing your performance on test day. As your foundation of content knowledge is built up and strengthened, you'll find that the strategies included in this chapter become more and more effective in helping you quickly sift through the distractions and traps of the test to isolate the correct answer.

Now that you're preparing to move forward into the test content chapters of this book, be sure to keep your goal in mind. As you read, think about how you will be able to apply this information on the test. If you've already seen sample questions for the test and you have an idea of the question format and style, try to come up with questions of your own that you can answer based on what you're reading. This will give you valuable practice applying your knowledge in the same ways you can expect to on test day.

Good luck and good studying!

Reading and Language

Comprehension Skills

Generating Questions About Texts Before, During, and After Reading

Asking questions during the process of reading is one way for you to become a more **active reader**. Active readers do not just sit back and have the content handed to them. Instead, they get involved with the text and are part of the process of learning. Asking questions before you read, pausing to ask questions while you're reading, and asking questions after you read are all good ways to help you become a more active reader. There are three types of questioning that can use as you try to think of questions.

Questioning Yourself

These are questions you ask yourself to see how well you're paying attention, and how involved you are in the story. Some example questions are

- Which character is my favorite so far?
- What do I think is going to happen next?
- Is there a character I am similar to in this story? Do I like those similarities?
- What would I do if I was in this situation?

Questioning the Author

Although the chances are slim that you will ever get the chance to meet most of the authors of the texts you read, another way to get involved in the text is to imagine that you are asking questions of the author him or herself. Some example questions are

- What did the author want me to see here?
- Why did he write about this subject?
- Why did the author use this phrase?
- What did she want the character to learn from this?

Questioning the Text

The last type of question you can ask to improve your reading is called questioning the text. To ask these questions, imagine that you are asking the text itself questions about how it works and what it means. Some examples are:

- What does this word mean?
- What is this paragraph describing?
- Why is this term used here?
- How does this sentence connect to the other sentences in this paragraph?

Predicting What Will Happen in a Story

When you read a story, you should look for clues to make a prediction about what will happen. At the end of the story, you may even think about what will happen next to the main character, and use the clues in the story to make a prediction. You can also use personal experience to help make a prediction.

Suppose there is a story about a boy going swimming, and he swims too far out. Suppose the story says the boy can't get back to shore and starts to yell. Suppose the lifeguard comes and helps him. Suppose the story stops after the boy goes back in the water again. The reader might make the prediction that the boy won't swim as far out this time. This may not be true, but it is the most likely thing to happen.

EXAMPLE

Describe what prediction can be made based on the following sentences:

> When Glen is sick, his mother keeps him home from school. He stays in bed all day and takes medicine. Glen woke up this morning with a sore throat. His head was hot, and he felt achy.

The story says that Glen's mother keeps him home when he is sick and that Glen spends the day in bed when he is sick. The story says that Glen woke up this morning with a sore throat. His head was hot, and he felt achy. The reader can figure out that Glen was sick. Because Glen's mother always keeps him home when he is sick, the reader can predict that Glen will be staying home from school and spending the day in bed.

You can also use text features find information to make predictions and verify conclusions determined about different texts. Using key words as clues, looking for bold print words, looking for sentences that include captions, and words that are written in italics are a few features that can be used to help understand and make predictions about a text.

USING STRUCTURE AND GENRE TO MAKE PREDICTIONS

The structure and genre of a story can also help readers make predictions. Most stories follow the same structure. They have an exposition, rising action, a climax, falling action, and a resolution. Because most stories follow this structure, readers can predict that each of these parts will occur in the story. For example, rising action usually begins after the conflict of the story is introduced. This means that if characters have not faced any conflict, the reader can predict that something will go wrong for the characters. Likewise, stories in the same genre may contain similar events. For example, in a mystery, the characters work to solve a crime or explain a strange event. So, when reading a mystery, the reader can predict that the conflict will be a crime or event that the characters must learn more about.

MAKING CONNECTIONS TO ENHANCE COMPREHENSION

Reading involves thinking. For good comprehension, readers make text-to-self, text-to-text, and text-to-world connections. Making connections helps readers understand text better and predict what might occur next based on what they already know, such as how characters in the story feel or what happened in another text. Readers can make connections before, during, and after reading. Venn diagrams and other graphic organizers can help readers visualize connections.

TEXT-TO-SELF

Reading while looking for connections with the reader's life and experiences makes literature more personally relevant and meaningful to readers. Sentences showing text-to-self connections may begin with these examples

- This reminds me of a time when...
- I understand how the character feels because...
- The setting makes me think of...
- I experienced this same thing when...

Text-to-Text

Reading while looking for connections to other texts helps the reader learn to identify the way authors use genre, setting, characters, plot elements, literary structure and devices, and themes to create meaning. Sentences showing text-to-text connections may begin with these examples

- The character in this story reminds me of the character in...
- These two stories are alike because...
- The conflict in this story is similar to the conflict in...
- The relationship between the friends in this story is different than the relationship in...

Text-to-World

Reading while looking for connections to the world helps the reader begin to see literature as a reflection of real life and notice patterns in history and current events. Sentences showing text-to-world connections may begin with these examples

- The event in this story sounds like the event in history when...
- The actions of this character sound like...
- This is like what happened in real life when...
- I heard about this on the news when...

Making Inferences

An **inference** is a **conclusion** or generalization that the reader makes based on the information provided within a text. Certain facts are included to help a reader come to a specific conclusion.

For example, a story may open with a man trudging through the snow on a cold winter day, dragging a sled behind him. The reader can infer from the setting of the story that the man is wearing heavy winter clothes in order to stay warm. Information is implied based on the setting of a story, which is why setting is an important element of the text. If the same man in the example was trudging down a beach on a hot summer day, dragging a surf board behind him, the reader would assume that the man is not wearing heavy clothes. The reader makes inferences based on their own experiences and the information presented to them in the story.

Readers may come to their own conclusion about a topic, or the author may state a conclusion at the end of a story. When readers are in the middle of a story, they can predict what will happen at the end of it based on the events that have occurred so far and the typical characteristics that have been presented by the author up to that point. A reader needs to consider all of the information that an author has presented, including the main point and supporting points, to make logical conclusions and inferences about the story.

Example

Describe what can be inferred from the following sentences:

> Sometimes after a big storm, the beaches are covered with dead fish, seaweed, broken shells, and pieces of wood. Most seaweed is brown or gold, but there are often pieces of white seaweed. If people visit the beaches, the white seaweed disappears very quickly. It makes a delicious pudding.

To make an inference a reader needs to look for clues in a text. The author does not tell an inference directly; the author hints at one. Here the text says that fish, seaweed, and shells are on the beach after a storm. It also says that some of the seaweed is white and adds that the white seaweed is used for pudding. Another clue is that the white seaweed disappears quickly if people visit the beaches. The inference that a reader can figure out is that the people take the seaweed. It disappears quickly because it can be used to make a delicious pudding.

EXAMPLE

Draw a conclusion based on the following sentence from "The Sing-Song of Old Man Kangaroo" by Rudyard Kipling:

> "He hopped through the Flinders; he hopped through the Cinders; he hopped through the deserts in the middle of Australia."

Based on the wording in the sentence, the character appears to be a kangaroo. The fact that the character hopped through the deserts in the middle of Australia lends the reader to believe that the character is a kangaroo. The reader needs to use personal knowledge of geography, animals, and context clues to draw this conclusion. The title of the story includes the word kangaroo, as well, which gives the reader a clue that the character described in the story is that type of animal.

Using context clues, or wording in a sentence, is an important way to identify what the author is talking about in the story. An author will often leave blanks for the reader to fill in on their own, using information that has been presented up to that point in the story.

KEY IDEAS AND SUPPORTING DETAILS

Identifying **key ideas** helps the reader see what a text or story is mostly about. They are the **most important ideas** in a text, and everything else in the text builds around and supports them. Every piece of writing has key ideas. The **supporting details** in a story, such as the characters, events, and settings, will work together to reveal the key ideas. The details are not key ideas, themselves. They make the key ideas clear and show the reader the author's purpose for writing the text.

Synthesizing a Text with Existing Knowledge

Synthesizing is similar to summarizing but it takes it one step further. Synthesizing involves taking the main points of a text and comparing it with existing knowledge to create a new idea, perspective, or way of thinking.

Example

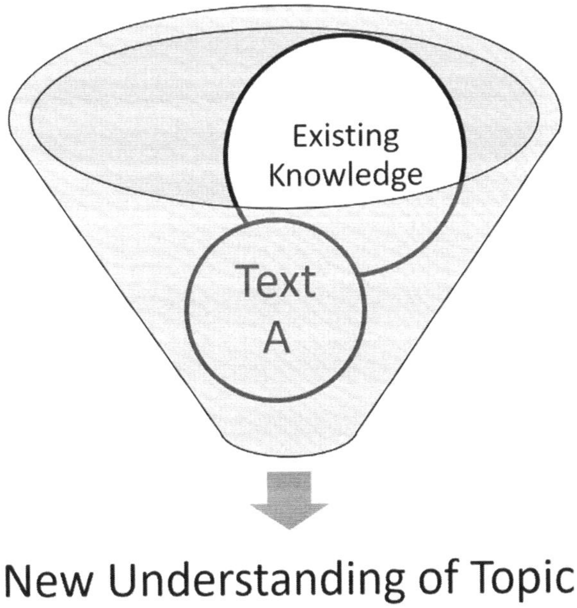

Another term for knowledge that you already have is **schema**. The plural form of this word is **schemata**. Schemata contain all the ideas you have about something. Synthesizing is all about how schemata change over time with the introduction of new information.

Using self-questioning strategies can help readers synthesize texts with their schemata to increase or change their understanding of topics. These questions include

- What do I already know about this topic?
- Is any of this new information?
- Has my perspective changed now that I've read this?
- What do I understand now that I didn't before?
- What are the main ideas of this text?
- How do the parts of the text fit together to create meaning?
- Are there any text-to-text, text-to-self, or text-to-world connections here?

Synthesizing Texts Without Existing Knowledge

If the reader is completely unfamiliar with the topic, they will have no background knowledge. In this case, instead of using existing knowledge, synthesizing may instead be done by combining the ideas provided in two or three different texts. The reader must make connections between the texts, determine how the ideas fit together, and gather evidence to support the new perspective.

Chapter Quiz

1. There are three types of questioning that you can use for active reading. What are these three types of questions?

a. Questioning the composition, grammar, and style of the writing
b. Questioning history, current events, and the future
c. Questioning your personal context, surrounding culture, and the world
d. Questioning yourself, the author, and the text

2. Which of the following helps the reader learn to identify ways authors use genre, setting, characters, plot elements, literary structure and devices, and themes to create meaning?

a. Reading while looking for connections to the reader's life
b. Reading while looking for connections to other texts
c. Reading while looking for connections to the world
d. Reading while looking for connections to history

3. Which of the following is a conclusion that the reader makes using clues in the text?

a. Thesis
b. Prediction
c. Inference
d. Guess

4. What term refers to knowledge that you already have?

a. Cognition
b. Glossary
c. Schema
d. Explicit information

Chapter Quiz Answer Key

1. D: See section **Generating Questions About Texts Before, During, and After Reading**

2. B: See section **Making Connections to Enhance Comprehension**

3. C: See section **Making Inferences**

4. C: See section **Synthesizing a Text with Existing Knowledge**

Response Skills

Text Evidence

The term **text evidence** refers to information found in a text that supports a reader's claim about the text. A reader can draw conclusions or inferences based upon information found in a text. Often, the author will deliberately include information that supports the main point of the text to help the reader make conclusions and inferences that align with the author's purpose for writing the text.

Drawing Conclusions Based on Text Evidence

Readers often need to use prior experience and background information to draw an accurate conclusion about the passage they are reading. Sometimes interpreting the information in a sentence can be difficult, especially if the reader is unfamiliar with some of the words used in a sentence. Looking at the words that the reader does understand in the sentence can help. By taking a pen or pencil and underlining important information in a sentence, the reader can better understand what the author is trying to say and draw a clearer conclusion from that.

Example

Draw a conclusion based on the following quote from *Flora & Ulysses: The Illuminated Adventures* by Kate DiCamillo.

> Take this squirrel, for instance. Ulysses. Do I believe he can type poetry? Sure, I do believe it. There is much more beauty in the world if I believe such a thing is possible.

This quote is from the character Dr. Meescham, who is speaking to Flora about her squirrel, Ulysses. Saying a squirrel can type seems silly, but the doctor says he does believe it's true. The phrase "there is much more beauty… if I believe" helps the reader draw the conclusion that Dr. Meescham encourages imagination, and that seeing the world as beautiful is important. The things characters say often show something important about them. Be sure to read dialogue carefully to see what conclusions the author might be wanting you to make.

Example

Read the following quote from *Shiloh* by Phyliss Reynolds Naylor and draw a conclusion based upon the information presented.

> Last of all, I take the lard bread from my pocket and feed it to Shiloh in little pieces, letting him lick my fingers after every bite. I wrap my arms around him, pat him, run my hands over his ears, even kiss his nose. I tell him about a million times I love him as much as I love my ma.

The reader can conclude that the narrator adores his dog Shiloh. The words "wrap my arms around him," "kiss his nose," and "tell him about a million times I love him" lead the reader to this conclusion. The reader can also assume that Shiloh loves the narrator as well because he allows all of the touches that he is receiving. Readers know from experience that animals do not often allow touch from people they do not have affection for.

When interpreting a sentence, always look for key phrases that can be used to draw conclusions about characters and their relationships. Authors carefully craft descriptions of each character to form a picture in the reader's mind about what the character is like.

Paraphrasing and Summarizing

Paraphrasing and summarizing are two ways readers can work to understand what they read. Both involve reading a text and recalling the main points in an accurate way, but they differ in several ways.

How to Paraphrase	How to Summarize
State the message in the text in the reader's own words, while keeping the original meaning of the text Take all of the original ideas and word them in a way that the reader can better understand Put what the reader has read into their own words, rephrasing what the author has written	State main points of the text clearly and to-the-point. Take information and state it simply, in a much shorter form. Put information in a short form that keeps the main points of the whole text. Do not include many details, just the main idea of the text

Paraphrasing is often done for individual ideas, while summarizing is done for an entire block of text or ideas. Often times, a summary can be done in just one sentence, boiling down the author's words into just main idea.

Review Video: Summarizing Text
Visit mometrix.com/academy and enter code: 172903

Paraphrasing the Main Point of a Sentence

Paraphrase the main point of the following two sentences:

> Emmanuel went swimming in the lake by his house, where the water reached a depth of twenty feet in the middle. He did not venture out more than six feet into the water, however.

When paraphrasing a couple sentences or an entire paragraph, always include the main point of the text being reviewed, this is what the reader needs to know about the text. In the example, the reader needs to know that Emmanuel went swimming in the lake, but not more than six feet out. A paraphrase of the text may include: Emmanuel went swimming six feet out in the lake by his house. That is the main point that the audience needs to know.

Recall that a paraphrase is stating the author's ideas in the reader's own words. A summary typically involves including the main points of a longer text, such as a novel or full story.

EXAMPLE

Read the following paragraph and then give a one sentence summary statement:

> When choosing a pet, people need to think about what type of home they can offer the animal. For example, a small apartment might not be a good fit for a large dog, but could be a comfortable home for a kitten. A house that has a big yard would be great for a puppy, but a rabbit does not need a large yard.

In order to summarize, one has to identify the main idea and any supporting ideas in the author's work. The summary is an overview of the author's paragraph and will tell what it is about without getting into any of the details. The summary needs to be broad enough to cover all of the information in the author's paragraph. Here is a possible summary statement for the above paragraph:

> People need to consider a number of factors when choosing a pet.

CHAPTER QUIZ

1. If a reader takes an author's original idea and then restates it, putting the idea into their own words, this is an example of:

a. Outlining text
b. Paraphrasing text
c. Summarizing text
d. Abstracting text

2. Which of the following is NOT true of summarizing?

a. A summary can be just one sentence that boils down the author's words into the main idea.
b. Summarizing helps readers work to understand what they have read.
c. A summary typically involves restating the main points of a text in a simpler, shorter fashion.
d. A summary should be subjective and include brief personal opinions on the subject.

CHAPTER QUIZ ANSWER KEY

1. B: See section **Paraphrasing and Summarizing**

2. D: See section **Paraphrasing and Summarizing**

Literary Elements

Theme

The **theme** of a story, essay, or poem is the lesson that it teaches, or the message the author wants to get across. The theme is linked to the characters, the setting, and the events in a story. Some themes are fairly common. These themes are called **universal themes** and they suggest things about life, society, and human nature.

The theme of a story is not the same as the topic of a story. The topic is what the story is about, but the theme is what a reader is meant to learn. Themes are very rarely stated in the text. Instead, the reader has to **infer** the theme by reading closely and thinking carefully about what the author is saying.

Themes are an important part of literature because they serve the purpose of teaching the reader or listener a truth about life. The theme is developed by how a character or characters respond to their situations and challenges.

Example

Read the following and consider the theme of the excerpt.

> Jeanie arrived at the bake sale early. She bought the biggest cake at the sale. Sally had to work late. When she finally got to the sale, no cakes were left. She got only two cookies. She was lucky to get anything.

The saying "the early bird gets the worm" is one way to explain the theme of the story. In the story we read that Jeanie arrived early at the bake sale and got the biggest cake. But when Sally arrived, all that was left were two cookies. The point of the story is that the early bird gets the worm—the worm in this case is a large cake. In this story, the topic is a bake sale, but the theme is not "bake sale" because the words "bake sale" do not teach the reader anything.

Characters

Character Trait

The traits of a character may include how they act and physical characteristics; a character trait is a behavior or physical characteristic that is unique to a specific character. For example, a character may be outgoing, which means he or she likes to talk a lot, or they may have bright red hair. These are both character traits.

An author uses character traits to describe a character in a story and help the reader to learn more about how the character acts and what they look like. By comparing the character traits in a story, the reader can see similarities and differences between characters. The author includes character traits to help the reader understand why a character may act a certain way in the story. For example, a character who is shy may not want to talk with a lot of people in a new classroom, but a character who is outgoing may want to talk with many people.

An author typically provides many details about a character so that the reader can learn more about the character's traits, motivations, relationships, and any conflicts they may have in the story. The traits of a character may include how they act and how they look. Characters are often motivated by things that have already happened in their life or how they feel about a topic. The author will often give the reader enough information about the character so that the reader can figure out why the character responds to a situation in a certain way. The author will also often give details about the relationships between characters and points they may conflict on. For example, a character may be good friends with another character; however, the two characters may disagree on where to play outside if one character likes being near the water and the other character does not.

Example

Read the following description of a character and decide, logically, whether the character is likely to go hiking outdoors:

> Jeremy lived in a high-rise in Chicago. He was studious, and not very athletic. Jeremy preferred to stay indoors and read a book, rather than enjoy outdoor weather.

Based on the description of the character's traits, preferences, and personality, he is not likely to go hiking outdoors. The description indicates that the character prefers reading, rather than enjoying outdoor weather. In addition, the character lives in a tall building in the middle of a large city, in order for him to enjoy the outdoors, he would have to travel away from where he lives. The character is not likely to change his preferences. A situation may lead the character to go hiking, but he is not likely to initiate the action on his own. A description of a character that is likely to go hiking outdoors may include a preference for outdoor activity and living near trails.

Character Relationships

A relationship is the way one character acts with another character in a story. The characters are often called **major characters** if they have a main part in the story and **minor characters** if they have a smaller part. There are many different kinds of relationships. For example, two children in a story may be friends, but they could be angry with each other, competing with each other, or helping each other. An author may tell the reader what kind of relationship the characters have. An author might give hints about a relationship. For example, the author may show one child making fun of the other child, which would suggest that the two children do not have a friendly relationship. The author might show one child teaching the other child how to read, which would suggest that the two children have a friendly relationship.

Example

Read the following sentences and describe the relationship Jill and Anna have:

> Jill came over to Anna and asked if she wanted an apple. "Sure, I'd love one. Thanks," Anna answered. Anna took a bite of the apple and started to chew it. Her chewing was so loud that they both started to laugh.

The author does not tell what the relationship between Jill and Anna is. The reader must figure it out from their actions. These actions are the clues the author gives. Jill asks Anna if she wants an apple. Anna says yes and starts to eat it. Her chewing is very loud. Both Jill and Anna start to laugh. They seem to like each other. Jill seems generous to Anna because she gives Anna an apple. They laugh together, and friends often laugh together. The reader can use personal experience to decide that it seems as though Jill and Anna are friends.

Characters' Feelings

An author can show how a character feels in many ways. For example, the character may laugh a lot, which shows that the character is happy. The character could cry, which shows that the character is sad. There are other ways an author shows a character's feelings. A character may say something that shows he or she is sad. For example, a character may say that she misses her old school. This statement would show that the character is sad. A character may say something about enjoying her new school. This statement would show that the character is happy. An author knows that a character's feelings are important in a story. Sometimes the author says how a character is feeling; other times the author gives hints or clues about what a character feels.

Example

Read the following sentences and describe how Lorna feels:

> Lorna walked forward very slowly. The strange scratching noise was growing louder. She thought about calling out for help, but she knew no one would hear her. She decided to keep going anyway.

The author does not tell the reader directly how Lorna feels, but there are many clues about how Lorna feels from her actions. The sentences say that Lorna walks forward slowly and that there is a strange scratching noise. The sentence also says that she thinks about calling for help. These clues all suggest that Lorna is frightened. She doesn't know what is making the scratching noise. She wants to call for help, but she cannot. She is scared. The sentences also suggest another feeling. Lorna doesn't run away. She decides to keep going. This is another clue. It shows that Lorna is also feeling brave.

Character Changes

Characters can change in a multitude of ways throughout a story; however, there are main aspects of a character that change. A character's identifying characteristics, such as personality or behavior traits, may change as the result of a prominent event in the story, current motivations, and conflicts. As conflicts change or are resolved, a character may no longer be motivated by striving toward a goal that was previously important to them. As the plot of a story moves along, characters can constantly change in relation to events that occur. Relationships between characters and the points of view of characters may change throughout a story as well.

Each story will have many different types of characters and each of these characters will have a different relationship with other characters. Stories usually have a protagonist, antagonist, and a variety of other characters including round, flat, and stock characters.

Protagonist

The main character in a drama, movie, novel, or other fictional text. The author portrays the protagonist in a way that the audience is most like to identify with themselves. The protagonist is generally undertaking some type of personal challenge throughout the story. The author writes the story so that the reader becomes aware of the protagonist's emotions and is generally able to empathize with the personal challenge.

Antagonist

The character that actively opposes the protagonist by trying to prevent them from succeeding. The antagonist is usually presented in such a way as to make the audience dislike them, and want them to fail at stopping the protagonist. The protagonist and antagonist oppose each other, so their relationship is almost always one of dislike.

Flat Characters

Does not have any substantial changes throughout the story. They stay the same despite the conflict, and do not learn any lessons. They are usually minor characters that might interact with the main character in some way.

Round Characters

Major characters in the story that will be more fully developed than other minor characters. They will usually encounter some type of conflict that they must overcome, and usually learn a lesson about life or themselves along the way.

Stock Characters

Often get their characteristics and mannerisms from stereotypes of people that are widely recognized. These types of characters are often repeated and well-known. Readers should be aware that stereotypes are rarely accurate in reality, and are generally intended to be humorous or dramatic. Some examples are evil stepmothers, unintelligent blondes, rude athletes, and loyal servants.

Plot

The term **plot** refers to the series of events that take place in a story. The events in a story may take place in one location or many, in a short amount of time or over many years. A story always has to start somewhere, and the first event in a story signals the beginning of the plot. Stories may vary in length from half a page to novel-length, but they all follow a progression of events that the author winds together to form the plot. The characters and events in the story determine what the plot will be. Readers may find a **plot line** useful as they try to put the events in the text in order and determine the relationships between events.

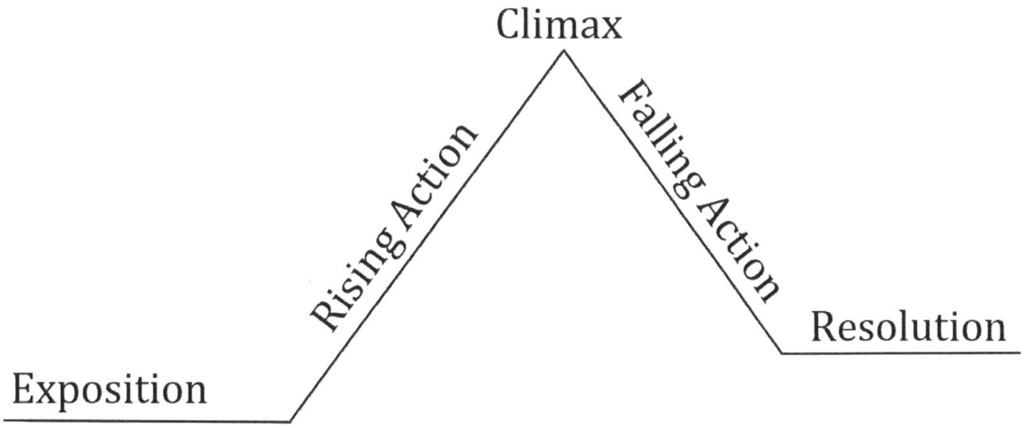

Review Video: Plot Line
Visit mometrix.com/academy and enter code: 944011

Every plot will begin with **exposition**, which introduces the characters and the setting of the story. The plot will continue to develop as new ideas and events centered on the main conflict in the story are revealed, which is called the **rising action**. The action in the story will rise until a **climax** is reached within the conflict. The climax can also be referred to as the turning point in the story, since the climax is where each character makes an important decision. After the climax, the action starts to wind down during the **falling action**. At this point, the characters begin to follow the paths they chose in during climax. The events of the story reach **resolution** in some way by the end of the story. Some conflicts are left open-ended, so that the reader is left to decide what really happened at the end of the story. Keep in mind that not all resolutions are happy or peaceful.

Example

Read the following plot and determine what the missing event is in the plot sequence:

> Sarita went to the store to buy eggs for her mother. She bought the eggs and got back on her bicycle to bring the eggs home. Her mother was angry that the eggs were all broken.

The reader has to guess based on the plot sequence what happened between events. The reader knows that Sarita got on her bicycle to go home. The reader also knows that the eggs were broken when she arrived at the house. Based on the context, the reader can assume that Sarita fell off her bicycle or dropped the eggs on the way home, causing them to all be broken when she arrived. The reader can assume that Sarita would have noticed if the eggs were already broken in the store. Plot often follows a logical sequence of events, but sometimes it is difficult to decide what actually happened between two events. In the example, the reader can logically assume that the eggs were broken on the way home.

Conflict

Conflict creates the basis for the plot of a story. A conflict may be between characters, a character and their own mind, or an outside influence. The main point of a conflict is that there is a problem that needs to be resolved. The problem may be a disagreement or an obstacle that has arisen and needs to be overcome.

An important part of analyzing the plot of a passage is identifying the **main conflict**. There will likely be many smaller conflicts in the story, but there will be one main problem that influences the characters and events. To identify the main conflict, first look at who the main character is. Now ask yourself what they want. They may want to something to happen or not happen, another character to do or not do something, or to confront or avoid a problem, among other things. Once you know what they want, now ask yourself what is standing in the character's way. It may be a person, an event, or something less tangible like the passing of time. Combining what the main character wants and why they do not currently have leaves the reader with a summary of the main conflict.

Example

Read the following sentence and explain the main conflict between the two characters:

> Joe stared angrily at Jamie's retreating back as Jamie raced away down the field with Joe's soccer ball.

The main conflict in the sentence is that Jamie has Joe's soccer ball. There may be additional conflicts between the two characters, but none are evident from the evidence shown in the sentence. In any story, a conflict may be minor and only affect part of the story, or be the main focus, taking an entire story to solve a conflict between characters. In the context of the sentence, it is not clear whether or not the entire story will revolve around Jamie taking Joe's soccer ball.

Resolution

The term **resolution** usually indicates the result of a conflict in a story. Conflict between characters, within a character, or against an external element is necessary in order to have a plot for a story. Without conflict, no events would occur to form the story. A conflict will come to a climax, and then conclude in some way. The resolution of a problem may be open-ended, end tragically, or end in a way that is good for everyone involved. The problem resolution typically occurs near the end of a story, after the climax has happened. A problem may be resolved by the characters involved within the conflict or by an external event; an upcoming resolution may be foreshadowed in the text, or may be completely unexpected by the reader. If the resolution is completely unexpected, it is considered to be a **twist** in the story.

Effect of Plot on a Story's Characters

The plot of a story unfolds as each event follows another, shaping the characters as they react to the various events that occur. Some characters are able to resolve their problems by the end of the story, while some characters fail to overcome their predicaments. As characters respond to the events around them, they reveal more and more about their personalities. Some grow and some do not. The reader can use the events of the plot to interpret the meaning of the story and understand its characters.

EXAMPLE

Read the excerpt and explain how finding the chest affects Marta.

> The map said this was the spot. Marta held her breath. Her fists were clenched into two tight balls. She lifted the shovel and scooped more sand out of the hole. There it was; she had found the chest with the diamonds. She opened the top. She would never need to work again. She smiled. It was really happening.

The event affects Marta by making her happy. The reader gets several clues that she is anxiously waiting ("Marta held her breath" and "her fists were clenched"), and that she is happy with what she found ("She smiled"). Events can cause characters to have all kinds of feelings. Here, something wonderful happened. However, events in stories are not always quite so happy. For instance, if a robber had suddenly seen Marta and the chest, he might have stolen the chest. That event would have had a very different effect on her. Readers need to pay attention to how characters are reacting to events, whether they are simply hinted at or stated in the story. In this way a reader will learn what characters are like.

SETTING

The setting is where a story **takes place**. The setting of a story may stay the same for the entire story, or change as events in the story unfold. For example, an entire story may take place in one room, or on the other end, a story could cross continents as the reader follows the characters along on a trail of events. Every story has to take place somewhere. The setting of story is described by the author in terms of what it looks like, how the character feels, and anything that is happening at that location at the time. For example, a character may be caught on a doorstep on a cold, rainy day. The character may feel frustrated as he shivers in the doorway, waiting for the heavy rain to let up a bit.

EXAMPLE

When listing ways that a story set in the city has a different backdrop from a story set in the countryside, answers will vary based on current knowledge of common characteristics for each setting. A story set in a city may be different from a story set in the countryside based on the following factors:

- Number of passersby: many people on a sidewalk vs. no other people around
- Background noise: car horns vs. bird calls
- Types of surroundings: tall buildings vs. fields of corn
- Types of transportation: subways and taxis vs. horses and farm trucks
- Daily activities being carried out: sitting at a desk in a skyscraper vs. plowing fields for planting
- Type of attire: a business suit vs. dirty jeans and boots

SHAPING A CHARACTER WITH SETTING OR PLOT

The setting of a story shapes character because it helps to define the situation that a character finds herself in. A character is limited to the setting of a story. For example, if a story takes place in a cold environment filled with snow and ice, this is certain to impact what actions a character can and will take. Frequently, the setting changes the way characters behave based on time. For example, the character of a woman who is a single mother in 1920 would be seen and behave very differently than a single mother in 2020.

Example

Read the excerpt and determine how the setting influences the character in this excerpt.

> She had swum too far out. The waves were higher than she thought. She was struggling hard to get to shore. She wondered if she would make it. She thought of her childhood. Had she been right to run away from home, she wondered? Just then, a lifeguard grabbed her and helped her to shore.

The setting of the ocean and the high waves creates a conflict in the character. She is worried. She thinks about her childhood and her parents. She doesn't know if she will make it to shore. This is how the setting affects the character in this excerpt. Without the high waves and the struggle, she would not become so worried and start to think about her past. She probably would not have questioned herself. This is an example of how a setting influences a character. If the waves had not been high, there probably would not have been a struggle or any self-searching of the swimmer's past.

Historical and Cultural Setting

Historical context influences literature in a number of ways. The style of the author's writing can be impacted by the historical period during which it was written (e.g., Dickens wrote at a time when authors were paid by the word; this is why his novels are so long). Obviously, the setting of the book includes its historical context. In addition, dialect may be a function of the historical period of the book. When a reader understands the historical context of a particular book, he or she can have a deeper understanding of the novel. Knowing about the time period during which the author wrote, as well as the time period discussed in the novel, helps the reader understand some of the author's choices, including character motivations.

Chapter Quiz

1. Which of the following is the lesson that a story teaches, or the message the author wants to get across?

a. Theme
b. Setting
c. Topic
d. Plot

2. What type of character often gets their characteristics and mannerisms from stereotypes of people that are widely recognized?

a. Minor characters
b. Stock characters
c. Flat characters
d. Round characters

3. Every plot will begin with __________, which introduces the characters and the setting of the story.

a. Conflict
b. Rising action
c. Foreshadowing
d. Exposition

Chapter Quiz Answer Key

1. A: See section **Theme**

2. B: See section **Stock Characters**

3. D: See section **Plot**

Literary Genres

Children's Literature

There are types of texts that are specifically meant to be read by children or younger audiences. Children's literature contains many different **genres**, which are categories that texts can be divided into. Some types of children's literature are

- **Folktales** -Songs, stories, myths, or proverbs belonging to a group of people. Often passed down from generation to generation by word of mouth.
- **Fairy tales** are stories that include fictional creatures or characters with fantastical traits and abilities. Fairy tales often end happily and depict the victory of good over evil. The plots and characters in fairy tales are often far-fetched and whimsical.
- **Fables** –Story told (often by a narrator) full of supernatural features like speaking animals. The tale demonstrates a useful truth at the end.
- **Legends** -A story featuring a national or folk hero. Often has a basis in actual fact, but also contains imaginative material.
- **Myth** -A legend or traditional narrative, often based on a historical event. The story reveals something about human behavior or the natural world, and often involves actions of gods.
- **Tall Tales** -A story full of outlandish exaggerations, often humorous and containing heroes who perform impossible acts easily.

Poetry

Poet Versus Speaker

The author of a poem is called a **poet**. Many poems are written in first person, which means the **stanzas** (groups of lines) include words like "I" and "me." However, the poet is not always the **speaker** of the poem. In a novel, the author can create characters with different points of view. The characters can argue or have different roles to play in telling the story. Similarly, a poet may write a poem from a different point of view or even include more than one voice. The speaker is the voice of the poem, and is not always the same person as the poet him or herself. The reader or listener should know that the person telling the story is a character, and not always a real person.

For example, this excerpt from a poem by Dr. Seuss reads:

> When you think things are bad,
> when you feel sour and blue,
> when you start to get mad...
> you should do what I do!
> Just tell yourself, Duckie,
> you're really quite lucky!
> Some people are much more...
> oh, ever so much more...
> oh, muchly much-much more
> unlucky than you!

Even though one line has the word "I" in it, the poem is not from the perspective of Dr. Seuss. He is the author of the poem, but not the speaker. The person saying "I" is a character, just like in a story.

Sensory Language in Poetry

Sensory language is when the author uses descriptive words and specific details that appeal to a reader's senses (sight, touch, taste, hearing, smell, emotion). For example, the author can use scents that the reader is familiar with to help them imagine what the setting of the poem smells and feels like. This use of sensory language is also called **imagery**.

Rhyme in Poetry

Poets use rhymes to help readers understand poems. Words **rhyme** when they sound similar to each other, especially when the similar sound is at the end of the words, like *cat* and *hat*, or *roar* and *soar*. Rhyming words usually have endings that are spelled the same way, but sometimes they are spelled differently, like *wait* and *hate* or *bear* and *snare*.

Famous poet Shel Silverstein uses rhyme in many of his poems. For example, in his poem "Listen to the Mustn'ts", the last word of the first- and second-lines rhyme with each other, and the last word of the third- and fourth-line rhyme with each other.

> Listen to Mustn'ts, child, listen to the Don'ts.
> Listen to the Shouldn'ts, the Impossibles, the Won'ts.
> Listen to the Never Haves, then listen close to me.
> Anything can happen, child, Anything can be.

The pattern of the rhymes in this poem forms a **rhyme scheme**. Sometimes poets use a rhyme scheme that makes every other line of the poem rhyme instead.

Drama

Dramas are texts that are written to be performed by people reading the lines or acting the stories out. They can also be presented as monologues (one character speaks), dialogues (two character speak to each other), or pantomimes (body movements are used instead of spoken words). Dramatic texts are called plays or **scripts**, and they are written differently than other texts.

Text Structure in Drama

Plays are divided into **acts** (large units) and **scenes** (small sections inside acts) instead of chapters. There are also **stage directions**, which are instructions from the playwright about where items go, where actors should move, and what the characters should be doing during the scene. Stage directions are usually in italics to set them apart from other parts of the play. When it is time for a character in a play to speak, there will be **character tag** on the left side of the page which shows the name of the character (all letters of the name are capitalized) followed by a colon.

Here is an example of how a page from a play might look:

Title of Play

Act Number

Scene Number

The setting of the scene is being described here. The reader is being introduced to the characters and the things happening around them. Characters will enter speak to one another during the scene.

CHARACTER 1:

I am speaking. These are words I say. *(stage directions)* I am still speaking.

CHARACTER 2 *enters and does something.*

CHARACTER 2:

Now I am speaking. This is my dialogue.

Dialogue and Stage Directions

Dialogue refers to what the characters say in a play when they are talking to each other, talking to themselves, or even talking to the audience. The type of speech, word choice, and accent a character uses is specific to the role he is playing. For example, a person cast to play a cowboy would have certain words in his vocabulary that a character from a big city in the North would not have.

A playwright also uses stage directions to make the play flow smoothly. Character interaction helps the viewer to understand the mood of the scene. If two characters are confrontational, the viewer is aware that there is some type of conflict occurring. Stage directions create order when all the characters are on stage together.

Informational Text

Controlling Idea

The controlling idea, also called the main idea or thesis, of a passage is usually located in the first paragraph or two of text. Having the controlling idea near the beginning of the passage allows the author to grab the reader's attention and let them know what the rest of the passage will discuss.

To find the controlling idea in a passage, there are questions the reader can ask while reading: What is this passage about? What does the author want the reader to know about the topic? The supporting details will provide evidence that the controlling idea is correct and are found in the body of a passage. The supporting details often provide examples of the controlling idea.

Supporting Details

Supporting details provide evidence and backing for the main point. All texts contain details, but they are only classified as supporting details when they serve to reinforce some larger point. Supporting details are most commonly found in informative and persuasive texts. In some cases, they will be clearly indicated with words like **for example** or **for instance**, or they will begin with words like **first**, **second**, and **last**. However, these special words are not a requirement. As a reader, it is important to consider whether the author's supporting details really back up his or her main point. Supporting details can be factual and correct but still not relevant to the author's point. Sometimes, supporting details can seem important but they might not support the main idea in the story well because they are based on opinion that cannot be proven.

Example

Read the following two sentences. State which sentence is a main idea and which sentence is a supporting detail. Explain the difference between the two sentences:

> She went fishing with her cousin Vinny.
> Jayden visited her relatives in Louisiana over the summer.

The first sentence is a supporting detail, and the second sentence is the main idea. A main idea gives the overall concept, or point, of the story. A supporting detail adds more information to the point of the story. The reader already knows that the name of the character needs to be introduced before using the pronoun she. Therefore, it makes sense that Jayden visiting her relatives in Louisiana over the summer must come before the supporting detail about her going fishing with her cousin Vinny. Once the reader knows the overall point of the text, supporting details help to explain what else happens in the story. The reader knows from the main point that the character Jayden is visiting her relatives in Louisiana, which is where she went fishing.

Structural Features of Informational Text

Texts which intend to inform the reader about a topic are often accompanied by visual aids or graphics. Some common examples are listed below.

- **Insets and sidebars** show additional information related to the text in boxes or on the sides of the page. Insets can contain pictures or text, and sometimes have different colored backgrounds or font types to make them stand out from the text.
- **Visual aids** include features like diagrams, graphs, and charts. These can help the user think about information in a different way. They do this by visually presenting the relationship between the information in the text.
- **Timelines** are a visual aid which show how events from the text happened over time, and usually contain dates, locations, or other related information.
- **Tables** are visual aids that organize information in a way that shows the relationship between the information. Tables are made using rows and columns, and the pieces in the rows and columns are called cells. Usually, the first row or column will contain a title or heading that categorizes or defines the other cells in that row or column.
- **Bullet points** list items separately, making facts and ideas easier to see and understand.
- **Numbers** can also be used to list separate items. Usually, numbers are used to show that the items are part of a sequence. For example, in a list of instructions, each instruction may be numbered to show the reader the order in which each instruction should be completed.
- **Italics** are a formatting technique that makes text appear slanted. Italics can be used to emphasize text because they cause the text to look different and lead the reader to notice it more easily. Italics are also often used in fiction to show that text is part of a character's thoughts. They are also commonly used to show that a word or section of text is written in a foreign language.
- **Boldface** is a way to format text to make it stand out. Boldface, or bold, text can be used to emphasize a word, phrase, or idea. Boldface can also be used to let the reader know that they can find more information about a term in a glossary, sidebar, or other feature of the text.

Organizational Patterns

Authors want to have an effective text that the reader can understand. If ideas do not follow a logical order, the reader will become confused and not know what the author is trying to say. When writing, there are a variety of ways that an author can choose to organize a written work. It is important to choose the pattern that best presents the information, as not all patterns will work for every piece of writing. An author may organize ideas according to a timeline, cause and effect, or description of an event or setting.

Order of Importance

The author puts the information in the text in order of what is most important. Order of importance can be either increasing or decreasing, depending on how the writer wants to structure the work.

Chronological Order

The author organizes the progression of events based upon when they occurred and what was included in each step of the story. By organizing the text in this way the author presents all necessary information about the six questions readers can ask to help themselves understand the text: who, what, when, where, why, and how.

Problem and Solution

The author presents some information as a problem and then discusses a solution or attempted solution to that problem. In problem and solution, there is generally one main problem, but that one problem may have several possible solutions.

For example, suppose Billy wants a new video game but does not have the money. There are several possible solutions to this. He might try asking his mom to buy it for him. If that does not work, he could offer to do small jobs to earn enough money to buy it. A third possibility might be to wait until his birthday and ask for it then.

Proposition and Support

The author states a proposition that they believe to be true, and then provides support for that proposition in the paper. The topics that use this type of structure are generally things that reader might feel uncertain about or might not already have an opinion about. The support that the author gives for the proposition should include facts, statistics, logic, and reasoning. The more hard evidence an author can give the reader, the better it will help convince them to see things from the author's point of view.

Cause and Effect

The author will write about relationship between two events that occur, where the second event occurs as a result of the first.

For example, a text may discuss a school policy stating that when a student is late to school too many times, they receive a detention. Later in the text, we might see a student repeatedly arriving late to school, after which he is given a detention. In this example, the **cause** is the student being late to school, and the **effect** is the student receiving a detention.

Compare and Contrast

The author will show similarities and differences between items or events.

For example, the author may write about cats and dogs. They might start by giving a brief description of the two. Then they will want to point out all of the similarities, such as; they both have tails, and both are kept as pets. Next, they will explain the differences, such as; dogs are canines, while cats are felines. They will try to provide as much detail as possible about both the similarities and the differences.

Identifying Organizational Patterns

Example

Read the following paragraph from a story. Describe how the author organizes information in the paragraph:

> First, John stopped at the grocery store to pick up some bread. Next, he went home and checked the mail. Finally, John sat down on the couch and opened up a book to where he had stopped reading.

The author uses chronological order to present information to the reader. The points in the story follow the order in which they occurred in time. The reader can look for words that give a clue as to progression of time, such as first, next, and finally. The paragraph does not use cause and effect, because one event does not lead to the occurrence of another. Each event is separate based upon when it occurred during the day. A progression of events can be placed on a timeline, to provide a visual image of when each event occurred. This is a helpful way to organize information in a lengthy story. The information in the paragraph is not overly descriptive, nor does it show where each event occurred in relation to another.

Example

Read the following paragraph from a news story and describe how the author organizes information in the story:

> The parade in honor of the town's 200th anniversary began at the corner of 57th Street at 9:00 a.m. on Saturday morning. Members of the fire department led the parade, dressed in their bright red hats and heavy yellow coats. At 9:15 a.m., members of the high school band gave a performance.

The news story uses chronological order organize ideas. The reader is given information about what type of event occurred, when the event occurred, what the event was about, and who was included.

Example

Identify organizational pattern that is used in the following sentence from *Morte d'Arthur* by Sir Thomas Malory:

> The king had given his promise, so he was obliged to agree.

The text structure of cause and effect is used in this sentence. The cause in the sentence is that the king gave his promise, and the effect is that he had to agree.

Argumentative Texts

Identifying the Claim

In a persuasive or argumentative text, the author is writing in order to make and support a claim. A claim is similar to the key idea of an informational text. However, a claim can be argued, which means that some readers may not agree with it. The author of the text will need to use the body of the text to support the claim and show readers why they should agree with it. To identify the claim of a text, first identify the topic. Then, read the introduction text to see what the author writes about the topic.

The claim should be clearly stated in the introduction. However, if the claim is still not clear, read the body to see what kind of evidence the author uses to support the claim. The way that the author gives and applies evidence may also show what the claim of the text is.

Call to Action

Another strategy is to look for a call to action in the text. A call to action is a statement that instructs the reader to do something after reading the text. Often, the call to action will tell the reader to do something that shows that he or she agrees with the author's claim. For example, if an author's claim is that reading is better than watching a movie, the author may include a call to action that says "Turn off the TV and dig in to a new book today!" By including this statement, the author is telling the readers to show their agreement by choosing to read rather than watch a movie.

Identifying How the Author Supports a Claim

In a persuasive or argumentative text, the author must use information to support his or her claim. This information is called evidence. Below are common types of evidence an author may use to support a claim:

- **Facts:** Authors may use facts that show that their claim is true. For example, a claim that fish are better pets than dogs can be supported by the fact that fish cannot make a mess inside a house.
- **Examples:** Authors may give examples of events or experiences that suggest that their claim is true. For example, an author may claim that people should exercise because it will make them healthier. The author could give an example of how exercise can improve a person's health in order to support this claim.
- **Quotes:** An author can support a claim by using quotes from other people or texts. If the person or text makes a statement that shows that the author's claim is true, the author can include that quote in his or her text. When authors include quotes in their work, they must always tell the reader where the quote came from.

The author must use enough evidence to support the claim. If the evidence does not fully support the claim in the text, then the author must continue working to find evidence for the claim. The evidence used to support a claim must also be believable and come from a reliable source.

Identifying the Intended Audience

Authors of persuasive and argumentative texts want to convince others to agree with a claim or take a certain action. Because of this, they will often write to a specific audience. Often, the target audience will include people who disagree with the author's claim. The author's desire is to give these people information that will lead them to change their minds or actions.

Strategies for Identifying the Intended Audience

One way to identify the intended audience of a persuasive or argumentative text is to first identify the author's claim. Then, consider who would disagree with the author's claim. This group of people is likely the group that the author wants to persuade.

Another way to identify the audience is to look for clues in the text. Sometimes, authors will clearly state which people are included in the intended audience. For example, imagine that an author includes the statement, "Teachers should reward their students every time they make a good grade on a test." This shows that the text is written to persuade teachers who do not already reward their students for good test grades. Similarly, a call to action may show who the target audience is by instructing the members of the audience to take a certain action.

CHAPTER QUIZ

1. What type of children's literature can be described as songs, stories, myths, or proverbs belonging to a group of people, that are often passed down from generation to generation by word of mouth?

a. Folktales
b. Fables
c. Legends
d. Tall tales

2. In dramatic texts (plays or scripts), which of the following are usually in italics to set them apart from other parts of the play?

a. Dialogues
b. Acts and scenes
c. Stage directions
d. Character tags

3. What structural feature is used to list items separately, making facts and ideas easier to see and understand?

a. Boldface
b. Bullet points
c. Sidebars
d. Headings

4. If an author writes about cats and dogs, showing their similarities and differences, this would be an example of what type of organizational pattern?

a. Cause and effect
b. Problem and solution
c. Proposition and support
d. Compare and contrast

CHAPTER QUIZ ANSWER KEY

1. A: See section **Children's Literature**

2. C: See section **Text Structure in Drama**

3. B: See section **Structural Features of Informational Text**

4. D: See section **Compare and Contrast**

Author's Purpose and Craft

Author's Purpose

An author may write a text for many different purposes. Four of the most common purposes are to inform, to persuade or influence, to express, or to entertain readers.

	Definition	Example
Informational Texts	Inform the reader on a topic that they previously knew nothing about, such as many non-fiction texts.	An informative paper on kangaroos would detail where kangaroos live, what they look like, what they eat, and other habits.
Persuasive Texts	Influence the reader to think a certain way about a topic, calling them to action or pointing them toward resources that would help them to learn more about the topic.	An author may try to persuade the reader that waterparks are the best place to go in the summer when it is hot outside. The author would present information about waterparks and explain *why* they are good places to visit.
Expressive Texts	Express the author or speaker's opinion or emotions about a topic. Lots of descriptive words are used to clearly show the reader how the author or speaker feels.	The author may think that a new playground in town is a good idea, and write an essay about why a playground would be great for the community.
Entertaining Texts	Entertain the reader, such as in most fictional texts.	Kate DiCamillo, the author of *Because of Winn Dixie*, entertains her readers with the story of a young girl named Opal and the stray dog who teaches Opal the meaning of friendship.

Authors usually write to entertain, to inform, or to persuade their readers. The organization structure or pattern they use is related to what the author's purpose is. It is important to choose the pattern that best presents the information, as not all patterns will work for every piece of writing.

Example

Read the following sentence. State the author's point in writing the sentence, whether it is to inform, persuade, express an opinion, or entertain:

> The rollercoaster reached a peak and paused for a second, before gliding down the other side of the hill with a roar.

The purpose of the sentence is to entertain the reader. The author does not state his or her opinion on the topic, and the sentence doesn't inform the reader about an important topic. The sentence does not persuade the reader to accept a certain point of view, and is instead meant to entertain the reader by giving them the feeling they might get from riding an exciting roller coaster.

Notice that the text describes an event, rather than an issue or conflict. The event is part of a larger tale, where a series of events occur to form an entire story. The reader may notice that the author uses descriptive words to present the setting, such as gliding and roar. The reader can better picture a story when the setting is clearly presented.

PRINT AND GRAPHIC FEATURES

An author may show information in a chart, a graph, in paragraph format, or as a list. Information may also be shown in a picture or a diagram. The way an author chooses to show information is often based on the purpose of the text and the audience that the text is meant to reach.

A reader may be asked to answer questions based on the graphic by itself, how the graphic relates to the text, or how the text would best be shown in a graphic form. Some common examples of graphics are cause and effect organizers, circle graphs, bar graphs, illustrations, and diagrams.

CAUSE AND EFFECT GRAPHIC ORGANIZERS

Cause-and-effect graphic organizers are often used to map the **elements of a story**. A reader might read a story about a string of events and then be asked to correctly fill in either the **cause** or **effect** of an event in the story.

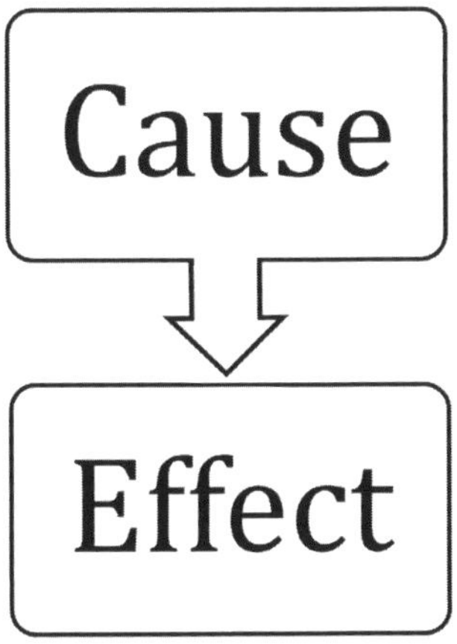

EXAMPLE

Read the following excerpt from *Ramona Quimby, Age 8* by Beverly Cleary and decide what the cause of the hectic morning at the Quimby house is.

> With all four members of the family leaving at different times in different directions, mornings were flurried in the Quimby household.

A **cause and effect** graphic organizer for this excerpt might look something like this:

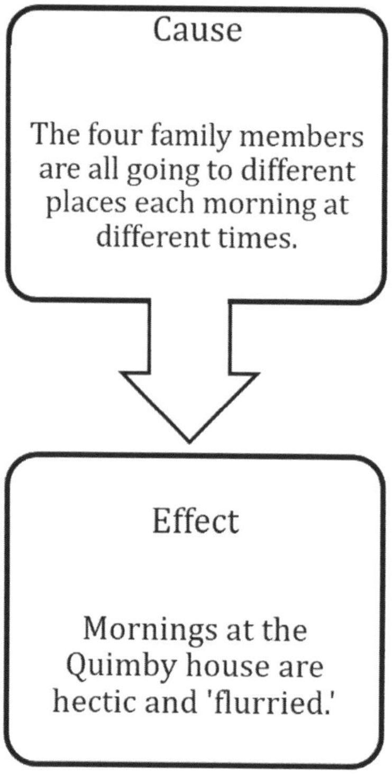

Circle Graphs

Circle graphs, also called pie charts, are often used to represent information that can be shown as **parts of a whole**. For example, this graph shows the results of people being asked about their favorite color:

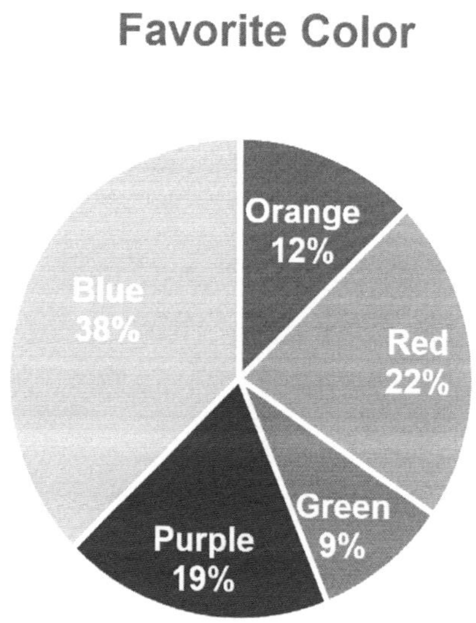

BAR GRAPHS

Bar graphs are used to show information about **numbers**. For example, this graph is a different way of representing the same results as those in the circle graph.

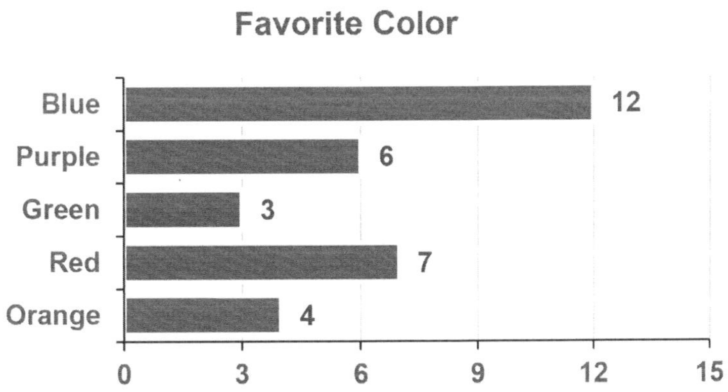

ILLUSTRATIONS AND PHOTOGRAPHS

Authors may choose to include **illustrations** or **photographs** (or both) with their texts. These two image types both show something from the text or give more information about the text.

Illustrations are drawings of an object. They may be based on reality, or they may represent an artist's abstract idea. For example, this is an illustration of a 1903 automobile:

Photographs are pictures of objects. They are generally extremely realistic, and most often show an object as it actually existed at that moment in time. For example, this is a photograph of a 1917 automobile:

Both illustrations and photographs give the reader another way to relate to and understand the text. The reader may be asked how the image relates to the text, what type of caption the image should be given, or why the author chose to include the image with the text.

DIAGRAMS

Diagrams are used to show information in a visual way. There are many different types of diagrams, including:

Diagrams that show the parts of an object, how they work together, or how they should be put together. This is an example of a diagram which shows how gears turn together

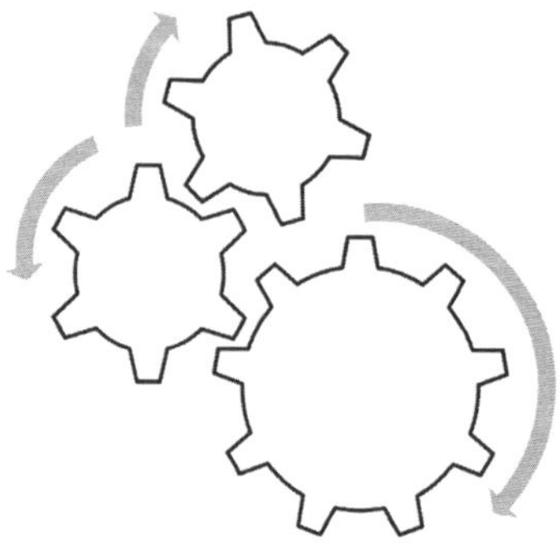

Diagrams that show how information is related are called **Venn Diagrams**. These are ways to visually see the way in which two different ideas overlap. This is an example of a Venn Diagram comparing cats and dogs:

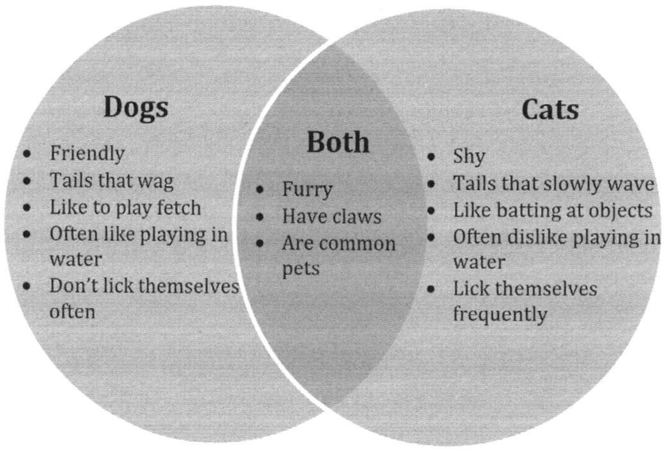

IMAGERY

Imagery is the use of **descriptive language** to add life or feeling to a work of literature. Many authors add literary and sound devices to create vivid pictures in the minds of their readers. Most of the time, imagery is thought to be one of the best ways to help readers fully understand and remember a work.

The most common forms of imagery are those that appeal to the sense of sight and sound. Imagery that appeals to the sense of sight, or **visual imagery**, helps the reader picture an event in their mind, usually by including specific details in the text that are not strictly necessary for the purpose of the story, but allow the reader to more easily "see" the scene. Some common forms of figurative language can help create visual imagery.

Review Video: Sensory Language Visit mometrix.com/academy and enter code: 177314

LITERAL AND FIGURATIVE LANGUAGE

Many types of text use both **literal language**, which means just what it says, and **figurative language**, which means something more than the literal words being used. Figurative language is a literary device that allows the author to expand reality in a vivid way. When an author uses figurative language, she connects things in an exaggerated way in order to create a memorable image, which helps to describe a situation in a new way for the reader.

Review Video: Figurative Language
Visit mometrix.com/academy and enter code: 584902

SIMILE

- Shows similarity between two ideas or objects, using the words "**like**" or "**as**"
- For example, an author might write "The princess is as beautiful as a rose" to compare the appearance of a woman to a beautiful flower.

METAPHOR

- Puts one idea in place of another to draw a parallel between the two ideas.
- For example, an author might write "Her room was a pigsty," to compare a person's bedroom to a dirty spot where pigs sleep.

HYPERBOLE

- An extreme exaggeration of an idea.
- For example, a character might say "I'm starving to death!" to show that they are really hungry. Most of the time a character who says this is not literally going to die from hunger, they are just ready for a snack.

IRONY

- Uses sarcasm or humor (usually with an emphasis on the opposite) to show difference from literal meaning.
- For example, if a character says "Well today must be my lucky day!" after they left their homework on the kitchen table, they are being ironic. The irony used here helps show that it is definitely *not* the character's lucky day.

PERSONIFICATION

- Gives life or human characteristics to an inanimate object
- For example, if an author writes "The trees whispered to each other across the wide blue sky," they are using personification to help the reader imagine the scene. Trees are not human beings, so they do not whisper, but the image created in the reader stands out more than a literal description would.

SOUND DEVICES

Sound devices allow authors to add another level to their texts by tapping into the spoken part of language. Authors may use many sound devices to create meaning and help readers understand them better, including:

Onomatopoeia

- Appeals to the reader's sense of hearing by using words that copy the noises objects or people make, like sound effects.
- For example, an author might write "The soccer ball whooshed across the field into the goalie's net, scoring the winning point!" The word "whooshed" is an **onomatopoeia** because it mimics the sound of air moving quickly. Because the writer chose to include an onomatopoeia, the reader is able to better picture the action in the sentence.

Alliteration, Assonance, and Consonance

- Alliteration, assonance, and consonance all deal with using the same sound throughout a line or sentence. **Alliteration** is the use of words that begin with the **same sound** in a sentence or in a line of poetry. **Assonance** refers to alliteration with a repeated **vowel** sound, whereas **consonance** refers to alliteration with **consonant** sounds.
- For example, the following line contains two sets of alliteration: "I saw a fly fly past my eye, straight into a fresh cherry pie. I felt a flea flee away from my knee and onto the sleeping dog." The first line uses the same sound in the words *I, fly, eye,* and *pie,* which is assonance. The second line uses both assonance and consonance, using the same vowel sound in *flea, flee, knee*, and, *sleeping*. The repeated consonants show up in the words *felt, flea*, and *flee.*

Review Video: Alliteration in Everyday Expressions
Visit mometrix.com/academy and enter code: 462837

Point of View

Authors choose which character tells the story they are writing. This is called **point of view**. The point of view affects the story in many ways. There are three general types of point of view:

First Person

- Tells a story through the eyes of one character.
- Uses the pronouns 'I,' 'me,' 'we,' and 'my.'
- The reader gets only one side of the story, without any other angles on what may have happened in the text

Second Person

- Tells a story using the pronoun 'you.'
- The least common point of view.

Third Person

- Tells a story about a character or group of characters from an outside viewpoint.
- Uses the words 'her', 'his,' 'they,' or a name to talk about a character or characters.
- A common way to show action in a story which allows the author to easily and realistically tell a story from more than one person's viewpoint.
- Gives readers a more complete view of a story as it is told from many different perspectives.

Anecdotes

Sometimes authors will use devices that are based on their own or others' experiences to try to make a text more believable or relatable. An **anecdote** is a brief story authors may use to help the reader relate to the author or his or her purpose for writing. Anecdotes can illustrate the author's point a way that is more real, believable, and relatable to the reader.

Style and Voice

Style and voice play an important role in the development of a story. The reader's impression of a story can vary based on the style and voice used by the author. **Style** refers to the way an author uses words, phrases, and sentence structure. The style of the text can change depending on whether the author uses short, choppy sentences, long, elaborate sentences, formal language, or informal language. **Voice** refers to the characteristics of a text that show the author's personality and distinguish the author from other writers. An author's voice may be recognized through the way they use words or the way they organize and present their thoughts. Voice is specific to each writer, and it can be as specific and unique as personality.

Chapter Quiz

1. An author's purpose in writing fiction is most often to:

a. Persuade
b. Inform
c. Entertain
d. Express

2. What is the least common point of view, that tells a story using the pronouns "you"?

a. First person
b. Second person
c. Third person
d. Narrator

3. What type of graphic can be used to visually see the way in which two different ideas overlap?

a. Circle graph
b. Bar graph
c. Venn diagram
d. Cause and effect organizer

4. What common form of figurative language puts one idea in place of another to draw a parallel between the two ideas?

a. Metaphor
b. Simile
c. Hyperbole
d. Irony

5. In poetry, which of the following appeals to the reader's sense of hearing by using words that begin with the same consonant sound in a sentence or in a line of poetry?

a. Assonance
b. Rhyme
c. Line breaks
d. Alliteration

6. What sound device appeals to the reader's sense of hearing by using words that copy the noises objects or people make (for example, pow or whoosh)?

a. Onomatopoeia
b. Alliteration
c. Assonance
d. Consonance

Chapter Quiz Answer Key

1. C: See section **Author's Purpose**

2. B: See section **Second Person**

3. C: See section **Diagrams**

4. A: See section **Metaphor**

5. D: See section **Alliteration, Assonance, and Consonance**

6. A: See section **Onomatopoeia**

Language

Vocabulary

Dictionary

A print or digital dictionary can be used to find out many things about a word. A dictionary will show the correct pronunciation of a word, provide its meaning, and identify what part of speech the word is. It will also tell how the word was derived—that is, what words it came from originally. A dictionary will have a **pronunciation guide** for each word that shows how to sound it out and where its syllables start and end. It will use symbols to indicate sounds, and will also use sample sounds (the "a" in "bad," for instance). A dictionary lists all of the meanings of a word and the parts of speech the word can be used as.

example \ ig-'zam-pəl\ noun

1. something that shows what a group of things is like
2. a model that should be either copied or avoided
3. a punishment meant to serve as a warning to others

Example:

Julia used her dictionary to check the various meanings of the word *clear*. She found this entry:

clear (klîr) adjective

1. obvious.
2. easily seen through
3. free from flaw or blemish
4. free from guilt; untroubled
5. out of the way
6. to tidy *v*
7. to free *v*
8. to earn *v*

Identify which definition of *clear* is used in the following sentence:

Janet stood *clear* of the crowd pushing to get through the door.

The correct answer is meaning 5: "out of the way." If you substitute that definition for the word, the sentence makes sense. Meanings 1, 2, 3, and 4 do not fit with the context of the sentence. Meanings 6, 7, and 8 are verbs and "clear" as it is used in the sample is an adjective. When considering which meaning is being used, always check for context clues in the sentence or in the sentences before or after the sentence in which the word is used.

THESAURUS

A thesaurus is a reference book that gives **synonyms** of words. It is different from a dictionary because a thesaurus does not give definitions. A thesaurus can be helpful in finding the meaning of an unfamiliar word when reading. If the meaning of a synonym is known, then the meaning of the unfamiliar word will be known. Another time in which a thesaurus can be helpful is when writing. Using a thesaurus helps authors to vary their word choice.

GLOSSARY

A glossary is a **list of terms and their definitions** that can be found **at the back** of certain types of books, such as textbooks or reference books. A glossary does not have the definitions of all words, like a dictionary, but instead gives the definitions of the important terms within that particular book which are either uncommon or newly introduced. One may use a glossary when reading a book about economics or a chapter in a science textbook, for example, to define some of the technical terms within the text.

USING CONTEXT TO DETERMINE THE MEANING OF WORDS

Readers of all levels will encounter words that they have either never seen or that they have seen before but still don't know what it means. The best way to define a word in **context** is to look for nearby words that can assist in learning the meaning of the word.

CONTEXT CLUES

Context clues are hints about the meaning of a word. They are the words or phrases in the sentence or sentences before and after a new or unfamiliar word. Context clues give the reader an idea about what a word means. A context clue may also contain words that help define the new word or an example of what the new word means. sing context clues to figure out meaning can be helpful when learning a new set of vocabulary words or reading a difficult text. The dictionary definition of a word can always be looked up to double-check intended meaning.

EXAMPLE

Read the following sentences and determine the meaning of the word *absorbed* based on context clues:

> Kamal was so *absorbed* by his video game that he didn't hear his grandmother calling him for dinner.

The dictionary definition of the word *absorbed* is "having one's attention fully engaged; greatly interested." In this sentence, the words "didn't hear" show that Kamal is not paying attention to anything other than what he's doing. The explanation that he's playing a video game tells us that he's most likely doing something he enjoys. The clues present in the sentence help the reader figure out that the word *absorbed* most likely means very interested. This word can also mean "liquid taken in or soaked up," but because Kamal is a person and not a liquid substance, the reader can determine that is not the correct meaning in this sentence.

SUBSTITUTION TO FIND MEANING

One way to find out if you have figured out the correct meaning of a new word is to **substitute** the meaning for the word. Using the example for *absorbed*, if the reader substituted in "very interested," the sentence would read

> Kamal was so "very interested" by his video game that he didn't hear his grandmother calling him for dinner.

This is a way for the reader to confirm that they have used the context clues in the sentence correctly.

Synonyms and Antonyms

When you understand how words relate to each other, you will discover more in a passage. This is explained by understanding **synonyms**, which are words that mean the same thing, and **antonyms,** which are words that mean the opposite of one another. As an example, *dry* and *arid* are synonyms, and *dry* and *wet* are antonyms.

Example

Read the following sentences and determine the meaning of the word *reluctant* based on context clues:

> Sam was *reluctant* to be in the play, so he told the director that he was too busy to rehearse and didn't go to tryouts. He felt too shy to get up on a stage.

In this example sentence, the words "too busy" show that Sam made an excuse about why he couldn't be in the school play. The sentence also says that he "didn't go to tryouts." The second example sentence has other clues. It says, "He felt too shy to get up on stage." These clues give the reader hints about what the word *reluctant* means. It means "not willing."

Multiple-Meaning Words

A multiple-meaning word has different **definitions** in the dictionary. Many words have multiple meanings, so the reader has to pay attention to how a word is used in a sentence to figure out which meaning is intended. A multiple-meaning word is spelled the same, no matter how it is used. So, to find the meaning of a multiple-meaning word, the reader needs to look at the information presented in the rest of the sentence. For example, look at the word *leaves* in the following two sentences:

- Michelle *leaves* the building at 5 o'clock every day.
- The *leaves* fell off the oak tree in September.

In the first sentence, *leaves* means exits. In the second sentence, *leaves* refers to parts of a tree. By looking at the rest of each sentence, the reader can understand which definition of the multiple-meaning word the author is referring to.

Example

Figure out the meaning of the multi-meaning word *part* from the context of the following sentence:

> Anita wanted to have a *part* in figuring out when the school trip would take place.

Possible meanings of the word *part* include "piece," "quantity," and "role." The example sentence says that Anita wanted to have a *part* in figuring out when the school trip would take place." If the reader substitutes each meaning of the word *part* for the word itself, the reader can figure out that the correct meaning is "role." It is the only word that makes sense in this example sentence. Anita wanted to have a role in figuring out when the school trip would take place. "Role" is the correct meaning of *part* as used here.

Example

Read the following sentence from *Charlie and the Chocolate Factory* by Roald Dahl and determine the meaning of the word *spellbound* based on context clues:

> "Little Charlie Bucket was staring at her absolutely *spellbound*, watching her huge rubbery lips as they pressed and unpressed with the chewing, and Grandpa Joe stood beside him, gaping at the girl."

In the context of the sentence, *spellbound* refers to not being able to turn away. The character Little Charlie Bucket is staring at a girl as she chews, which means that he is looking at her without moving. The character Grandpa Joe is looking at the girl as well, while standing right next to Charlie. The reader can decide, based on the sentence, that the two characters are viewing something unusual and do not want to look away. Even if the reader does not know the meaning of an unfamiliar word, looking at the surrounding sentence or sentences can help the reader to figure out the meaning.

Root Words, Prefixes, and Suffixes

The root, prefix, and suffix are parts of a word. The **root** is the main part of a word. It is what a **prefix** or **suffix** is attached to. A prefix goes on the front of a root word to make a new word. A suffix goes on the end of a root word to make a new word. Some words have both a prefix and a suffix. Many words have one or the other. The root, prefix, and suffix all have different meanings. By studying the parts of a word, the reader can figure out the meaning of a word.

Here are some common Greek Root words:

Root	Meaning	Example
auto	self	automobile (a self-propelled vehicle)
graph	writing	graphic (are, especially involving drawing or lettering)
meter	measure	thermometer (an instrument for measuring temperature)

Here are some common prefixes:

Prefix	Meaning	Example
mis-	wrongly	misspell (to spell wrongly)
sub-	under	submerge (to sink below the surface)
dis-	not	disagree (not agree)
pre-	before	preview (to view before)

Here are some common suffixes:

Suffix	Meaning	Example
-it/ity	state of	activity (state of being active)
-ful	full of	wonderful (full of wonder)
-er	a person connected with	teacher (a person connected with teaching)
-able	can be done	likeable (can be liked)
-ment	result of	payment (the result of being paid)

Example

Using current knowledge of prefixes and suffixes, determine the meaning of the word *misjudged* in the following sentence:

> After seeing him stop to help someone who had tripped, Tiffany realized she may have *misjudged* the new student.

A reader may know that *judge* means to make a decision. The prefix *mis-* means wrongly. Putting the entire word together, the reader can see that *misjudged* means to make a decision that is wrong. This makes sense in the context of the sentence. When people make quick decision about another person without knowing them long, they are more likely to judge them incorrectly. By paying close attention to the meaning of a root word plus any prefixes and suffixes, the reader can figure out what the author is trying to say.

Example

Figure out the meaning of *harmful* from its word parts.

> *Harmful* is made up of a root and a suffix. The root is *harm.* The word *harm* means "to hurt." The suffix is *-ful.* This suffix means "full of." A reader can figure out that the meaning of *harmful* is "full of hurt or harm."

Synonyms, Antonyms, Homophones, Homographs, and Idioms

Synonyms and Antonyms

Synonyms are words that have similar or the same meaning. For example, *happy* and *glad* mean the same thing, so they are synonyms. A word may have many synonyms. Other synonyms for *happy* are *content* and *pleased.*

Antonyms are words that have opposite meanings. For example, *big* is an antonym for *small.* A word may have many antonyms. Other antonyms for *little* are *large* and *huge.*

Here are some common words with possible synonyms and antonyms:

Word	Synonym	Antonym
Fast	Quick	Slow
Loud	Noisy	Soft
Pretty	Beautiful	Ugly
Rich	Wealthy	Poor
Sick	Unwell	Healthy
Start	Begin	End
Tired	Sleepy	Energetic

Review Video: What are Synonyms and Antonyms?
Visit mometrix.com/academy and enter code: 105612

Example

Determine if there is a synonym or an antonym for the word *silly* in the following sentence:

> Danny was so silly that his teacher had to keep reminding him to be serious and stop fooling around.

To figure out if there is a synonym for *silly*, the reader needs to look at the context of the sentence. A synonym means the same as another word. Danny's teacher reminds him to "stop fooling around." The sentence also says that Danny "was so silly." The term *fooling around* means almost the same as *silly*. The reader can tell this from the context clues because context clues are hints. An antonym means the opposite of another word. The teacher tells Danny "to be serious." The reader can figure out that *serious* means the opposite of *silly*. The reader can tell that *serious* is an antonym of *silly* because the context gives clues about the meaning of *serious* and *silly*.

Homographs and Homophones

There are several types of words that sound alike but that have different meanings. **Homographs** are words that are spelled the same way, but have different meanings and that aren't always pronounced the same way. **Homophones** are words that sound alike, but are spelled differently and have different meanings.

Because some words have many meanings, the reader has to decide which meaning of the word is being used. To figure out which meaning is being used, the reader needs to look for context clues to find hints about the meaning of the word. For example, the word *spot* is a homograph. It can mean "a place" or "a stain or blot." In the sentence "After my lunch, I saw a spot on my shirt," the word *spot* means "a stain or blot." Context clues help the reader figure this out. The hints include "lunch" and "on my shirt."

Homographs

Homographs	
Quarter	
It's a quarter past noon.	I put a quarter in the vending machine.
Bat	
I love to watch bats fly through the sky.	I had practice today, but I forgot my bat.
Left	
Look both right and left before you cross the road.	The plane left for New York at three o'clock.

Homophones

Homophones	
Bare	Bear
The trees already look bare.	These parks are full of bears.
Blue	Blew
My favorite color is blue.	My coffee was too hot, so I blew on it.
Reign	Rain
The kingdom wished the new queen a long and prosperous reign.	My garden will keep drying up is we do not get some rain soon.

Idioms

Idioms create comparisons, and often look like similes or metaphors. An **idiom** is a phrase that has a meaning that is different from the literal meaning of its individual words. For example, "break a leg" is a common idiom that is used to wish someone luck or tell them to perform well. Literally, the phrase "break a leg" means to injure a person's leg, but the phrase takes on a different meaning when used as an idiom. Another example is "call it a day," which means to temporarily stop working on a task. The phrase does not mean to literally refer to something as "a day."

Chapter Quiz

1. A thesaurus can do all of the following, EXCEPT:

a. Give synonyms of words
b. Give word definitions
c. Help find the meaning of an unfamiliar word
d. Help authors vary their word choice when writing

2. Which of the following are words that sound alike, but are spelled differently and have different meanings?

a. Synonyms
b. Antonyms
c. Homophones
d. Homographs

Chapter Quiz Answer Key

1. B: See section **Thesaurus**

2. C: See section **Homographs and Homophones**

Spelling

Vowels and Consonants

Vowels and consonants describe the sounds in the English language. **Vowels** are the sounds made with only the voice, such as /a/, /e/, /i/, /o/, and /u/. Sometimes the letter y can make an /i/ sound. Consonants make up all of the other sounds in English. Consonants are sounded out by using the tongue, teeth, and lips.

Syllables

Syllables are the individual sounds that make up spoken words. Syllables can be determined by saying a word out loud and listening to what the individual sounds are. Some people split sounds up differently, but the important part of syllables is knowing where each sound in a word starts and stops.

One Syllable	Two Syllable	Three Syllable	Four Syllable
Bat	Draw-ing	Ba-tter-y	Com-for-ta-ble
Car	Foot-ball	Com-put-er	In-vis-i-ble
Home	Wa-ter	Flam-in-go	Wat-er-mel-on

Sometimes, words are diagrammed using the letters v and c to describe the vowels and consonants in the word. This helps to determine what types of syllables the word contains.

	Closed Syllables	Open Syllables	VCe Syllables
Word	Cat	Banana	Ripe
Pronunciation	/Kat/	/Buh-Na-Nuh/	/Rīp/
Syllables	CVC	CV-CV-CV	CVC

Notice how in the first example, cat is one syllable, which is made up of a consonant sound from the letter c, a vowel from the letter a, and another consonant sound from the letter t. In the second example, banana is three syllables, each of which has a consonant followed by a vowel.

Closed Syllables

Closed syllables are the easiest to recognize. They are marked by a consonant sound closing off the beginning or end of a syllable.

Open Syllables

Open syllable refers to the beginning or end of a syllable that does not have a consonant closing it off. Examples of this include the words *egg* and *blue.* The number and placement of consonants in different open syllables can affect the way the vowel is pronounced in each syllable.

	VCCV	VCV
Word	Tennis, Method	Robin, Tiger
Pronunciation	/Ten-is/, /Meth-od /	/Rob-in/, /Tī-ger/
Syllables	VC/CV, VCC/V	VC/V, V/CV

VCe Syllables

VCe syllables refer to words that have a silent e in them. The letter e is included to help identify the word when reading it, but the e sound is not spoken. Examples of words with silent e sounds are *bite*, *cake*, *flute*, and *tube*.

VV Syllables

When two vowels appear next to each other in a word, they may work together to make a single sound. However, when the vowels do not make one sound together, they mark the end of one syllable and the beginning of another syllable. These are VV syllables, also called vowel teams. For example, *duel*, *flour*, and *diary* all contain VV syllables.

R-Controlled Vowel Syllables

R-controlled syllables are formed when an *r* comes after a vowel. In r-controlled syllables, the vowel is paired with the *r* and makes a unique sound. Examples of words with r-controlled syllables are *jar*, *teacher*, *fir*, *torn*, and *spur*.

Final Stable Syllables

When a word ends in a Cle syllable, or a consonant followed by *le*, it has a final stable syllable. The syllable is made of these three letters. Examples of words with final stable syllables are *spectacle*, *thimble*, and *giggle*.

HOMOPHONES

Homophones are words that sound the same when spoken aloud, but which have different definitions. **Homophones** are usually spelled differently. Below is a list of common homophones.

Word 1	Word 2	Word 3
Allowed	Aloud	
Ate	Eight	
Be	Bee	
Blew	Blue	
Board	Bored	
Cell	Sell	
Dear	Deer	
Eye	I	
Here	Hear	
Hour	Our	
Its	It's	
Knot	Not	
Night	Knight	
Mail	Male	
Pair	Pear	Pare
Plane	Plain	
Right	Write	
Road	Rode	
Some	Sum	
Sun	Son	
There	Their	They're
Two	To	Too
Way	Weigh	
Week	Weak	
Whole	Hole	

COMMONLY MISSPELLED HOMOPHONES

TO, TOO, AND TWO

To can be an adverb or a preposition for showing direction, purpose, and relationship. A dictionary can also be used to see the many other ways to use *to* in a sentence.

Examples: I went to the store. | I want to go with you.

Too is an adverb that means *also, as well, very,* or *in excess.*

Examples: I can walk a mile too. | You have eaten too much.

Two is a number.

Example: You have two minutes left.

There, Their, and They're

There can be an adjective, adverb, or pronoun. Often, *there* is used to show a place or to start a sentence.

> Examples: I went there yesterday. | There is something in his pocket.

Their is a pronoun that is used to show ownership.

> Examples: He is their father. | This is their fourth apology this week.

They're is a contraction of *they are.*

> Example: Did you know that they're in town?

Knew and New

Knew is the past tense of *know.*

> Example: I knew the answer.

New is an adjective that means something is current, has not been used, or is modern.

> Example: This is my new phone.

Its and It's

Its is a possessive pronoun that shows ownership.

> Example: The guitar is in its case.

It's is a contraction of *it is.*

> Example: It's an honor and a privilege to meet you.

Your and You're

Your is a pronoun that shows ownership.

> Example: This is your moment to shine.

You're is a contraction of *you are.*

> Example: Yes, you're correct.

EXAMPLE

In the passage below, choose the correctly spelled word from each pair in parentheses.

> My grandparents gave me a (knew/new) raincoat when I visited them yesterday. It was the perfect gift because it started raining when I left (their/there) house! The rain was very heavy, but the raincoat kept me (drie/dry) and warm. When I got home, I wrote and mailed them a letter to thank them for (their/thier) useful gift.

The first set of words is *knew* and *new*. Remember that homophones are words that are spelled differently but sound the same when spoken out loud. These words have different meanings, so it is important to choose the correct homophone carefully. In this sentence, the word is being used to describe a raincoat, so it must be an adjective. *Knew* is the past tense form of the verb *know*, while *new* is an adjective. *New* is the correct choice for the first set of words.

The next set of words is *their* and *there*. This is another set of homophones! Remember what each spelling means. *There* is most commonly used to show location, and *their* is a possessive pronoun. How is the word used in the sentence? It comes before *house* and tells who the house belongs to. Since *their* is used to show ownership, it is the correct choice in this set.

The third set of words is *drie* and *dry*. One of these words is spelled correctly, while the other is not. Remember that every word must have at least one vowel, and *y* can sometimes act as a vowel. There is not always a rule for when a word should end in *ie* or *y*, so this is an example of a word that should be memorized. *Dry* is the correct spelling.

The final set of words is their and thier. Remember the rule for spelling words that use *e* and *i* together. In this set, there is no *c* and the vowels do not make a long *a* sound together. The *i* must come before the *e* in this case, so *their* is the correct choice.

AFFIXES AND ROOT WORDS

Affixes are syllables attached to the beginning or end of a word to adjust its meaning. Both prefixes and suffixes are affixes. A **prefix** is a syllable that appears at the beginning of a word that adjusts the root, or base, word' s meaning. For example, the prefix *mis* means wrong. When combined with the root word *spelling*, the word *misspelling* is created, which means wrong spelling. A **root word** is the base of a word that can have affixes added to it. For example, the suffix *-er* can be added to the root word *manage* to create *manager*, which means a person or thing who manages. The suffix *-able*, meaning capable of, can be added to *manage* to create *managable*, which means capable of being managed. Keep in mind that not every prefix and suffix can be simply added to a root word, since adding an affix will sometimes require some other spelling changes for the root word.

Common Prefixes

Prefix	Definition	Examples
anti-	against, opposing	antigravity, antidote
com-	with, together, very	community, combine
de-	from	depart, detangle
dis-	away, off, down, not	dislike, disappear
ex-	out	extract, exterior
inter-	among, between	intersection, interstate
mis-	bad, poorly, not	mistake, misspell, misunderstand
non-	not	nonexistent, nonsense
over-	above, in excess	overdone, overhead
post-	after, following	postpone, postscript
pre-	before, previous	prevent, premade
pro-	forward, in place of	propel, pronoun
retro-	back, backward	retrospect, retrograde
semi-	half, partly	semicircle, semicolon
sub-	under, beneath	submarine, subject
super-	above, extra	superstore, supervise
re-	backward, again	repeat, redo
trans-	across, beyond, over	transform, transport, transit
un-	not, reverse of	unhappy, unlock
uni-	one	uniform, unity

Common Suffixes

Suffix	Definition	Examples
-able or -ible	capable of being	suitable, edible
-ation	action, state, result	occupation, federation, starvation
-dom	state, rank, condition	kingdom, wisdom
-en	cause to be, become	deepen, strengthen
-er or -or	role, function	teacher, elevator
-ess	feminine	waitress, actress
-ful	filled with, marked by	thankful, hateful
-hood	state, condition	falsehood, statehood
-ion	action, result, state	union, confusion
-ish	suggesting, like	feverish, childish
-ist	worker, status, follower	dentist, finalist, colonist
-ity or -ty	state, quality, condition	ability, faulty
-ize	cause to be, treat as	realize, emphasize
-less	lacking, without	hopeless, countless
-ment	result, action	refreshment, employment
-ness	quality, state	greatness, dullness
-ous	marked by, given to	religious, gracious
-ship	status, relationship, trait	penmanship, friendship

Spelling Changes with Suffixes

When a suffix is added to the root word, usually the resulting word is spelled just like the root word and the suffix put together. However, there are some words that will require other spelling changes when a suffix is added. These changes include doubling consonants, removing *e*, and changing *y* to *i*.

DOUBLE CONSONANTS

Most words that end in a closed syllable with one closing consonant will need the final consonant doubled if a suffix is being added.

Adding -ing: fibbing, submitting, running

Adding -er: sadder, flipper, hummer

Adding -est: biggest, flattest, hippest

REMOVING E

Many words ending with a VCe syllable will lose the silent *e* when a suffix is added. This only applies if the first letter of the suffix is a vowel.

ROOT WORDS ENDING IN Y

If the root word ends with a consonant and a *y,* when a suffix is added, an *i* will replace the *y.*

Adding -ness: silliness, readiness, stickiness

Adding -ous: glorious, studious, industrious

Adding -ed: applied, satisfied, spied

COMMON SPELLING MISTAKES

VOWELS

There must be a vowel in every word. If a writer spells a word without a vowel, he or she has made a mistake and should correct it. Not every word needs a consonant, and there are even some words that are made of one vowel, like *a* or *I*. If a word has more than one syllable, there should also be at least one vowel in every syllable. However, there are words and syllables that do not contain *a*, *e*, *i*, *o*, and *u*. In these words and syllables, *y* acts as a vowel.

I BEFORE E

If a word contains the letters *i* and *e* right next to each other, the *i* usually goes before the *e*, such as in *relieve*. However, if the two letters come right after a *c*, then the *e* should go before the *i*, such as in *receipt*. Also, if the two letters make a long *a* sound when spoken aloud, the *e* should go before the *i*, such as in *their*. Several words do not follow these rules, so it is best to double-check the spelling of confusing words in the dictionary.

CHAPTER QUIZ

1. Which of the following words has three syllables?

a. Invisible
b. Battery
c. Drawing
d. Football

2. When a word ends in a Cle syllable, or a consonant followed by *le* (for example, spectacle, thimble, or giggle), it has what type of syllable?

a. VCe syllable
b. VV syllable
c. Final stable syllable
d. R-controlled syllable

3. All of the following prefixes can mean "not" EXCEPT for:

a. dis-
b. ex-
c. non-
d. un-

4. When adding a suffix to most words that end in a closed syllable with one closing consonant (for example, sad or flip), what change needs to be made to the root word?

a. No change is needed
b. Add a y before the suffix
c. Add a silent e
d. Double the final consonant

5. If a word contains the letters *i* and *e* right next to each other, the *i* usually goes before the *e*, EXCEPT when the two letters come right after:

a. C
b. F
c. N
d. T

6. There, they're, and their are commonly misspelled homophones. Which one is a pronoun that is used to show ownership?

a. There
b. They're
c. Their
d. All of the above

Chapter Quiz Answer Key

1. B: See section **Syllables**

2. C: See section **Final Stable Syllables**

3. B: See section **Common Prefix**es

4. D: See section **Double Consonants**

5. A: See section **I Before E**

6. C: See section **There, Their, and They're**

Writing Process

Brainstorming

When choosing what to write about, activities like brainstorming can help inspire new ideas or help writers see how their ideas go together. **Brainstorming** means considering a variety of topics or ideas and is mainly used to find a creative approach to a subject or problem. A good first step in brainstorming is simple **free-association** with a topic. One way of doing this is sitting down with paper and pen and writing every thought that comes to mind about the topic in a word or phrase. It does not matter how helpful or good the thought seems at first; the writer should write down everything that comes to mind about the topic. Then, the writer should read the list over a few times. Next, he or she should look for patterns, repetitions, and clusters of ideas. This allows a variety of fresh ideas to come as the writer thinks about the topic.

Free Writing

Free writing is a more organized form of brainstorming. **Free writing** means taking a limited amount of time, like 2 to 3 minutes, to write everything that comes to mind about a topic in complete sentences. When the time is up, the writer should review everything he or she has written down. Many of the sentences may not make sense, but they may contain ideas and details that help the writer organize his or her ideas and prepare to plan the composition. Usually, free writing results in more useful ideas than brainstorming because the writer's thoughts and connections are written in complete sentences. However, both methods can be used together to help the writer prepare to plan and write a composition.

Mapping

One specific way to use graphic organizers is to map an essay. There are many different types of graphic organizers. One easy method to create one is to draw a circle in the middle of the page and write a broad topic in it. Then, draw smaller circles with related topics and ideas, or with topics that fit within the broad topic, written inside and draw line to connect each circle to the main circle. This method can show ideas that fit within the broad topic and will help guide the essay, or it can show which ideas may work better as the main topic of the essay.

Once the main idea and other ideas and details for the essay have been chosen, they can be used to map the essay. Mapping is another word for using a certain type of graphic organizer. These graphic organizers look like a map and organize ideas and details as they will appear in the essay. The essay map can have the main idea at the top or in the center. If the main idea is at the top, the supporting ideas will appear below it in a row, and any additional details will appear under the supporting idea they go with. If the main idea appears in the center, the supporting ideas may appear around it, and the additional details will appear around the supporting ideas they go with.

Planning

Planning is the process of organizing a piece of writing before writing a draft. At the beginning of planning, writers should decide **why they are writing** and **who will read what they write**. The writer must also choose a **genre**, which is the **type** of composition he or she will write. There are fiction genres, such as comedy, folklore, action, and mystery. There are also nonfiction genres, such as essays, reports, poems, and journals. To plan his or her composition, a writer may create an outline or a graphic organizer, such as a Venn diagram, a spider-map, or a flowchart. These methods should help the writer choose their topic, main ideas, and how to organize the composition. If the writer needs to do research for the composition, he or she may also do so as they plan. Planning helps writers organize all of their ideas and decide if they have enough information to begin their first draft. However, writers should remember that the decisions they make during planning may change later, so their plan does not have to be perfect.

Drafting

Writers may then use their plan, outline, or graphic organizer to compose their first draft. They may write more drafts after the first one to improve their writing. Writing multiple drafts can help writers think of different ways to state their ideas and correct mistakes that may be hard to fix without rewriting a section of the composition, or the whole composition. There is no "right" number of drafts, so different writers may write a different number of drafts. Writing drafts also makes it easier to write freely because a writer can improve his or her composition with each draft they write.

Revising, Editing, and Proofreading

Once a writer completes a draft, he or she can move on to revising, editing, and proofreading to improve the draft. **Revising** is making sure that the composition is right for the audience, is not missing important information, is on topic, and is well organized. Revising may happen after the first draft so that errors are not repeated in the next draft. Each draft should be revised before the next one is written so that no mistakes are missed. **Editing** comes next. Editing a composition includes steps like improving transitions between paragraphs and making sure each paragraph is on topic. While editing, the writer must pay attention to the words he or she uses and the way the information in each paragraph is organized. Writers may also fix grammar mistakes in the editing phase, since some errors will require a writer to rewrite large parts of their work. **Proofreading** means fixing misspelled words, errors in grammar, and any other small mistakes in the composition.

During the revising, editing, and proofreading steps, it can be helpful for writers to ask a peer to read their work, since he or she may notice mistakes or problems the writer missed before. A writer may also choose to read his or her own work aloud, or listen to someone else read it. Hearing a composition aloud can help writers find mistakes or opportunities for improvement in their work more easily. This happens because when something is read aloud, the person reading the text must pay closer attention to the words on the page. When a writer or a peer reads the composition, they should point out any sentence that confuses them the first time they read it. Most of these sentences can be revised in a way that makes it easier to read and understand.

Adding and Removing Information

While both revising and editing may involve changing the words in a composition, they can also involve adding or taking away words. When a writer has completed a draft and reread it, he or she may notice that something, such as a transition, important details, or an explanatory sentence, is missing. Simply changing the words to make the passage sound better will not solve this problem, so the writer must **add** whatever words and information is needed to make the passage make sense and achieve the writer's purpose.

In other cases, a writer may have words, a sentence, or sometimes an entire paragraph that gives unnecessary information or explains the information in a way that is confusing. When this happens, the extra words and information weaken the composition and must be **removed**. Sometimes, this is difficult for writers to do because it may require them to remove writing they are proud of or a fact they find interesting. Despite this, revising and editing are steps meant to improve and strengthen a composition, so the writer should change, add, or remove parts of his or her writing in a way that makes it better and achieves his or her purpose.

Revising Sentences

Sentence variety is important to consider when writing an essay. A variety of sentence lengths and types can make an essay more engaging, and different types of sentences can sometimes help readers better understand information. For example, a sentence containing a list may make more sense when written with a simple sentence structure, since writing a compound sentence containing a list may give the reader too much information at once. On the other hand, information that is closely related and can be connected with a conjunction should be written in a compound sentence, rather than a simple sentence, since a compound sentence helps the reader see that the information goes together.

Using only simple sentences often makes writing boring and bothersome to read. Writing using only compound sentences makes it difficult for writers to explain information well and difficult for readers to understand, since every sentence will include a coordinating conjunction. To check an essay for sentence variety, it is helpful to look at whether the essay contains different sentence structures and lengths. It is also important to pay attention to the way each sentence starts and avoid beginning with the same words or phrases.

Revising Vocabulary

When writing informational or argumentative texts, it is important to use **precise vocabulary**, or **word choice**, to explain your main idea and supporting details. Generalized vocabulary will not help the audience fully understand the points that you are attempting to make because it will not accurately explain your main idea and supporting details. Precise vocabulary is important to use because it will accurately describe the ideas that are central to your text. When you research a subject, make sure to familiarize yourself with any vocabulary that is involved in its explanation. Use context clues, dictionaries, or, if necessary, a technical dictionary to decode any words that you are not familiar with. Precise vocabulary also impacts the effectiveness of narrative text. Carefully choosing vocabulary to describe sensory details, or imagery, helps writers paint the best possible picture of the events they are describing through their writing.

Chapter Quiz

1. Which of the following means taking a limited amount of time, like 2 to 3 minutes, to write everything that comes to mind about a topic in complete sentences?

a. Brainstorming
b. Drafting
c. Mapping
d. Free writing

2. What is often the first step after a writer completes a draft, and involves making sure that the composition is right for the audience, it is not missing important information, is on topic, and is well organized?

a. Adapting
b. Editing
c. Proofreading
d. Revising

3. When revising sentences in an essay, which of the following is NOT good advice?

a. Avoid beginning sentences with the same words or phrases
b. Include a variety of sentence lengths
c. Improve understanding by only using compound sentences
d. Keep sentences simple when they include lists

4. In what step of the writing process does the writer decide why they are writing, who will read what they write, and what genre they want to write?

a. Brainstorming
b. Drafting
c. Mapping
d. Planning

Chapter Quiz Answer Key

1. D: See section **Free Writing**

2. D: See section **Revising, Editing, and Proofreading**

3. C: See section **Revising Sentences**

4. D: See section **Planning**

Essay Structure and Organization

Controlling Ideas and Supporting Details

In the first paragraph of a composition, writers include a sentence that explains the **controlling idea.** The rest of the paragraph shows the reader why the topic of the essay is interesting and includes details that support the controlling idea. One way to understand the relationship between the controlling idea and supporting information is to think about a table: the tabletop is the controlling idea, and each of the table's legs is a supporting detail or group of details. All of the legs work together to support the tabletop and create a table, just like the supporting details work together to support the controlling idea and create a composition.

Introduction

The introduction is used to capture the reader's attention and announce the essay's controlling idea. Normally, the introduction contains about 3-5 sentences. An introduction can begin with an interesting quote, a question, a strong opinion, or something else that will **interest** the reader's and prompt them to keep reading. If the composition has a prompt, the introduction should **restate** or **summarize** some part of the prompt so that the reader will have an idea of what information will be in the essay. Finally, your introduction should include the **controlling idea**, the primary thing the essay will tell the reader.

Review Video: Introduction
Visit mometrix.com/academy and enter code: 961328

Body

In an essay's introduction, the writer states the controlling idea and prepares the reader for the information in the rest of the composition. In the body of the composition, the writer **explains**, **demonstrates**, and **gives more information about** the **controlling idea**. This is done using supporting details and examples that are relevant to the controlling idea of the composition. For example, if the composition's controlling idea is a vacation the writer took, the body will include descriptions of where the writer went, what they experienced, and what they thought of the trip. If the composition's controlling idea is the writer's opinion, the body will include examples and facts that show why he or she has formed that opinion. If composition's controlling idea is a topic and the writer wants to instruct the reader, the body will contain facts, explanations, and examples that help teach the reader about the controlling idea. A writer will use supporting details to explain the controlling idea throughout the body.

The body should also contain multiple paragraphs, and the order the writer puts these paragraphs in is important. Each paragraph should include at least one supporting detail, but a paragraph may include more than one if two or more supporting details work together to support the controlling idea. If the controlling idea is to describe something that happened, the paragraphs should match the order in which the events occurred. If the controlling idea is to present an opinion or instruct the reader, the paragraphs should be ordered in the way that would make the most sense to the reader. The order of body paragraphs is important because it can impact how easy a composition is to read.

Review Video: Drafting Body Paragraphs
Visit mometrix.com/academy and enter code: 724590

Paragraphs

After the introduction of a passage, the body paragraphs will explain and elaborate upon the controlling idea. While each paragraph should relate to the controlling idea of the composition, each paragraph should focus on one point or supporting detail. Normally, a paragraph has a good topic sentence that summarizes the paragraph's main point. A topic sentence is a sentence that gives an introduction to the paragraph and its contents. Topic sentences should contain information that is more specific than what is in the introduction and may include a supporting detail, but they should not contain explanations or examples.

Supporting Details

The next sentences in the paragraph should support the topic sentence. These sentences can contain examples, explanations, or other specific information that supports the topic sentence, which supports the controlling idea of the composition. While a paragraph may be structured in any way, as long as it logically provides information that supports the controlling idea, it can be best to use a template or pattern to make sure that each paragraph is complete and well organized. For example, a good template to follow is topic sentence, evidence, explanation, conclusion. This means that after the topic sentence, the next sentence should provide evidence, such as a quote or example, that shows that the supporting detail is true or relevant. Next, the paragraph should include a sentence that explains how the evidence supports the paragraph's main point. If there are multiple examples or quotes, more than one sentence may be used for each section. Finally, there should be a sentence that concludes the paragraph. The concluding sentence may be similar to the topic sentence, but it should help the reader understand the paragraph and prepare them for the next one.

Length of a Paragraph

A paragraph must contain enough information to support its main point and the composition's controlling idea. A paragraph of two or three sentences will most likely not support the main point or controlling idea because it is not likely to contain enough information, explanation, or evidence. When a paragraph does not support the main point or controlling idea, it does not help the writer achieve their purpose or goal for writing the essay. A helpful, informative paragraph will often have somewhere from three to five sentences.

Starting a New Paragraph

For most forms of writing, you will need to use multiple paragraphs. This means that deciding when to start a new paragraph is very important. Reasons for starting a new paragraph include:

- To separate the introduction and conclusion from the body paragraphs
- To move from one supporting detail or point to another
- To indicate an important shift in time or place
- To show a comparison, contrast, or cause and effect relationship

Transitions

Transitions between sentences and paragraphs guide readers from idea to idea and show relationships between sentences and paragraphs. Writers should use transitions carefully and only when they are truly helpful. They should also be selected to fit the author's purpose. Transitions can show relationships such as time, comparison, an order of events, and cause and effect. Transitions are often used at the beginning of a phrase, sentence, or paragraph, since this helps prepare the reader for the next piece of information.

Types of Transitional Words

Time	Afterward, immediately, earlier, meanwhile, recently, lately, now, since, soon, when, then, until, before, etc.
Sequence	too, first, second, further, moreover, also, again, and, next, still, besides, finally
Comparison	similarly, in the same way, likewise, also, again, once more
Contrasting	but, although, despite, however, instead, nevertheless, on the one hand... on the other hand, regardless, yet, in contrast.
Cause and Effect	because, consequently, thus, therefore, then, to this end, since, so, as a result, if... then, accordingly
Examples	for example, for instance, such as, to illustrate, indeed, in fact, specifically
Place	near, far, here, there, to the left/right, next to, above, below, beyond, opposite, beside
Repetition, Summary, or Conclusion	as mentioned earlier, as noted, in other words, in short, on the whole, to summarize, therefore, as a result, to conclude, in conclusion
Addition	and, also, furthermore, moreover

Review Video: Transition Words
Visit mometrix.com/academy and enter code: 707563

Conclusion

The conclusion of a composition should summarize the controlling idea and show that it has been explained well. A good conclusion shows the reader why the author's controlling idea is meaningful and important and how the supporting details should help the reader understand the controlling idea. The conclusion should also give the reader something to think about that is related to the controlling idea. For example, in the conclusion, the author can invite readers to think about how they feel or what they think after reading the composition. Some things to avoid when writing conclusions include:

- Introducing a completely new idea
- Apologizing for one's opinions or writing

- Repeating the controlling idea word for word rather than summarizing them
- Using the conclusion to summarize every detail in the composition

Review Video: Drafting Conclusions
Visit mometrix.com/academy and enter code: 209408

Chapter Quiz

1. "Too," "and," "next," "still," "besides," and "finally" are all what type of transitional word?

a. Time
b. Sequence
c. Comparison
d. Contrasting

2. Which of the following should be avoided in an essay conclusion?

a. Reminding the reader of the central idea by repeating it word for word
b. Showing the reader why the author's central idea is meaningful and important
c. Showing that the central idea has been explained well
d. Giving the reader something to think about that is related to the central idea

3. A helpful, informative paragraph will often have how many sentences?

a. One to three sentences
b. Three to five sentences
c. Five to ten sentences
d. Ten to fifteen sentences

4. The body of an essay should do all of the following, EXCEPT:

a. Introduce the central idea
b. Demonstrate the central idea
c. Explain the central idea
d. Give information about the central idea

Chapter Quiz Answer Key

1. B: See section **Types of Transitional Words**

2. A: See section **Conclusion**

3. B: See section **Length of a Paragraph**

4. A: See section **Body**

Grammar

SUBJECTS AND PREDICATES

SUBJECTS

Every sentence needs a subject and a predicate. The **subject** of a sentence names who or what the sentence is about. The subject may be directly stated in a sentence, or the subject may be implied. The **complete subject** includes the simple subject and any **modifiers**, such as adjectives, articles, prepositions, and adverbs, that go with it. To find the complete subject, ask *Who* or *What* before the verb to complete the question. The answer, including any modifiers, is the complete subject. To find the **simple subject**, remove all of the modifiers in the complete subject.

Examples:

simple subject

The small, red car is the one that he wants for Christmas.

complete subject

simple subject

The young artist is coming over for dinner.

complete subject

Review Video: Subjects in English
Visit mometrix.com/academy and enter code: 444771

An imperative sentence is a sentence that gives someone instructions or makes a request to someone. In **imperative** sentences, the verb's subject is understood, but is not actually present in the sentence. For example, this about the sentence *Drive to the store*. This sentence is a command, and the subject is *you*. If the subject were directly stated, the sentence would be *You, drive to the store*. Another fact to consider is that, normally, the subject comes before the verb. However, the subject comes after the verb in sentences that begin with *There are* or *There was*.

Direct:

John knows the way to the park.	Who knows the way to the park?	John
The cookies need ten more minutes.	What needs ten minutes?	The cookies
By five o'clock, Bill will need to leave.	Who needs to leave?	Bill
There are five letters on the table for him.	What is on the table?	Five letters
There were coffee and doughnuts in the house.	What was in the house?	Coffee and doughnuts

Implied:

Go to the post office for me.	Who is going to the post office?	You
Come and sit with me, please?	Who needs to come and sit?	You

Predicates

In a sentence, there is always a predicate and a subject. The subject tells what the sentence is about, and the **predicate** explains or describes the subject.

Think about the sentence *He sings.* In this sentence, we have a subject, *He*, and a predicate, *sings.* This is all that is needed for a sentence to be complete. Most sentences contain more information, but if this is all the information that is given in a sentence, then it is a complete sentence.

Now, let's look at another sentence: *John and Jane sing on Tuesday nights at the dance hall.*

subject: John and Jane | predicate: sing on Tuesday nights at the dance hall.

John and Jane sing on Tuesday nights at the dance hall.

Subject-Verb Agreement

Verbs **agree** with their subjects in number. In other words, singular subjects need singular verbs. Plural subjects need plural verbs. **Singular** is for **one** person, place, or thing. **Plural** is for **more than one** person, place, or thing. Subjects and verbs must also share the same point of view, as in first, second, or third person.

Review Video: Subject-Verb Agreement
Visit mometrix.com/academy and enter code: 479190

Number Agreement Examples:

Single Subject and Verb: Dan (singular subject) calls (singular verb) home.

Dan is one person. So, the singular verb *calls* is needed.

Plural Subject and Verb: Dan and Bob (plural subject) call (plural verb) home.

More than one person needs the plural verb *call.*

Person Agreement Examples:

First Person: I *am* walking.

Second Person: You *are* walking.

Third Person: He *is* walking.

Complications with Subject-Verb Agreement

Words Between Subject and Verb

Words that come between the simple subject and the verb do not affect subject-verb agreement.

Examples:

singular subject — singular verb
The joy of my life returns home tonight.

The phrase *of my life* does not affect the verb *returns.*

singular subject — singular verb
The question that still remains unanswered is "Who are you?"

Don't let the phrase "*that still remains…*" confuse you. The subject *question* goes with the verb *is.*

Compound Subjects

A compound subject is formed when two or more nouns joined by *and*, *or*, or *nor* act together as the subject of the sentence.

Joined by And

When a compound subject is joined by *and*, it is treated as a plural subject and requires a plural verb.

Examples:

plural subject — plural verb
You and Jon are invited to come to my house.

plural subject — plural verb
The pencil and paper belong to me.

Joined by Or/Nor

For a compound subject joined by *or* or *nor*, the verb must agree in number with the part of the subject that is closest to the verb.

Examples:

subject — verb
Today or tomorrow is the day.

subject — verb
Stan or Phil wants to read the book.

subject — verb
Neither the pen nor the book is on the desk.

subject — verb
Either the blanket or pillows arrive this afternoon.

Indefinite Pronouns as Subject

An indefinite pronoun is a pronoun that does not refer to a specific noun. Different indefinite pronouns are used as a singular noun, a plural noun, or change depending on how they are used.

Always Singular

Pronouns such as *each*, *either*, *everybody*, *anybody*, *somebody*, and *nobody* are always singular. This is because these pronouns always stand in for one person, place, or thing.

Examples:

singular subject — singular verb
Each of the runners has a different bib number.

singular verb — singular subject
Is either of you ready for the game?

Note: The words *each* and *either* can also be used as adjectives. For example, *each* person is unique. When one of these adjectives modifies the subject of a sentence, it is always a singular subject.

singular subject — singular verb
Everybody grows a day older every day.

singular subject — singular verb
Anybody is welcome to bring a tent.

Always Plural

Pronouns such as *both*, *several*, and *many* are always plural. This is because these pronouns always stand in for more than one person, place, thing, or idea.

Examples:

plural subject — plural verb
Both of the siblings were too tired to argue.

plural subject — plural verb
Many have tried, but none have succeeded.

Depend on Context

Pronouns such as *some*, *any*, *all*, *none*, *more*, and *most* can be either singular or plural depending on what they are representing in the context of the sentence.

Examples:

singular subject — singular verb
All of my dog's food was still there in his bowl.

plural subject — plural verb
By the end of the night, all of my guests were already excited about coming to my next party.

Example

Which word should go in the blank?

Joan and Susan ____ going to the store this evening.

a. Is
b. Are
c. Am
d. Was

Try using each choice in the sentence. Choice A, *is*, forms this sentence: Joan and Susan is going to the store this evening. There are two people, Joan and Susan, who are going to the store. This makes the subject of the sentence plural. *Is* is a singular verb, meaning it does not agree with the subject and cannot be the answer.

Choice B, *are*, forms this sentence: Joan and Susan are going to the store this evening. The subject of the sentence is still plural. But *are* is a plural verb! The subject and verb agree, so *are* is the correct answer.

Choice C, *am*, forms this sentence: Joan and Susan am going to the store this evening. *Am* is a singular verb, and it is also only used in first person, when the writer or speaker is referring to themself. The subject is plural, and the sentence is in third person, so *am* is not the correct answer.

Choice D, *was*, forms this sentence: Joan and Susan was going to the store this evening. *Was* is a singular verb, so it does not agree with the plural subject in this sentence.

Complements

A complement is a noun, pronoun, or adjective that is used to give more information about the subject or verb in the sentence.

Direct Objects

A direct object is a noun or pronoun that takes or receives the **action** of a verb. A complete sentence does not need a direct object, so not all sentences will have them. When you are looking for a direct object, find the verb and ask *who* or *what.*

Examples:

I took *the blanket.*

Jane read *books.*

INDIRECT OBJECTS

An indirect object is a word or group of words that show how an action had an **influence** on someone or something. If there is an indirect object in a sentence, then you always have a direct object in the sentence. When you are looking for the indirect object, find the verb and ask *to*, *for*, *whom*, or *what*.

Examples:

We taught [the old dog]^(indirect object) [a new trick.]^(direct object)

I gave [them]^(indirect object) [a math lesson.]^(direct object)

Review Video: Direct and Indirect Objects
Visit mometrix.com/academy and enter code: 817385

PHRASES

A phrase is a group of words that functions as a single part of speech, usually a noun, adjective, or adverb. A **phrase** is not a complete thought, and does not contain a subject, but it adds detail or explanation to a sentence, or renames something within the sentence.

CLAUSES

A clause is a group of words that contains both a subject and a predicate (verb). There are two types of clauses: independent and dependent. An **independent clause** contains a complete thought, while a **dependent (or subordinate) clause** does not. A dependent clause includes a subject and a verb, and may also contain additional information, but it cannot stand as a complete thought without being joined to an independent clause. Dependent clauses function within sentences as adjectives, adverbs, or nouns.

Example:

[I am running]^(independent clause) [because I want to stay in shape.]^(dependent clause)

The clause *I am running* is an independent clause: it has a subject and a verb, and it gives a complete thought. The clause *because I want to stay in shape* is a dependent clause: it has a subject and a verb, but it does not express a complete thought. This is due to the fact that it begins with *because*, which shows that there is more information needed to complete the thought. This dependent clause adds detail to the independent clause to which it is attached.

SENTENCE STRUCTURE

Sentence structure is based on the type and number of clauses in the sentence. Two common sentence structures are simple sentences and compound sentences:

SIMPLE

A simple sentence has one independent clause with no dependent clauses. A simple sentence may have a **compound subject** or a **compound verb**, or both.

Examples:

single subject: Judy | single verb: watered

Judy watered the lawn.

compound subject: Judy and Alan | single verb: watered

Judy and Alan watered the lawn.

single subject: Judy | compound verb: watered | compound verb: pulled

Judy watered the lawn and pulled weeds.

compound subject: Judy and Alan | compound verb: watered | compound verb: pulled

Judy and Alan watered the lawn and pulled weeds.

COMPOUND

A compound sentence has two or more independent clauses with no dependent clauses. Usually, the independent clauses are joined with a comma and a coordinating conjunction or with a semicolon.

Examples:

independent clause: The time has come | independent clause: we are ready

The time has come, and we are ready.

independent clause: I woke up at dawn | independent clause: the sun was just coming up

I woke up at dawn ; the sun was just coming up.

Review Video: Sentence Structure
Visit mometrix.com/academy and enter code: 700478

EXAMPLE

Which of the following could be added to the end of this sentence to change it from a simple sentence to a compound sentence?

I went for a walk last night.

a. Because I was not tired
b. With my sister
c. And I saw a shooting star
d. Since the weather was nice

This sentence is a simple sentence, since it contains only an independent clause. To become a compound sentence, the sentence must contain two or more independent clauses, and these independent clauses should be joined by a coordinating conjunction. So, a good way to answer this question is to find the answer choice that contains a coordinating conjunction and is an independent clause.

Choice A forms this sentence: I went for a walk last night because I was not tired. While *I was not tired* is an independent clause, it is joined by the word *because. Because* is not a coordinating conjunction, and it causes this choice to be a dependent clause. Choice A is incorrect.

Choice B forms this sentence: I went for a walk last night with my sister. *With my sister* is actually not a clause at all, since it does not have a subject and predicate. Choice B is a phrase, so it is incorrect.

Choice C forms this sentence: I went for a walk last night, and I saw a shooting star. Because this sentence has an independent clause followed by another independent clause with a coordinating conjunction, a comma has been added after the first clause. This also means that this sentence is a compound sentence! Choice C contains a coordinating conjunction and is an independent clause, so C is correct.

Choice D forms this sentence: I went for a walk last night since the weather was nice. While *the weather was nice* is an independent clause, it is joined by the word *since. Since* is not a coordinating conjunction, and it makes this choice a dependent clause. This means choice D is incorrect.

Sentence Fragments

Recall that a group of words must contain at least one **independent clause** in order to be considered a sentence. If it doesn't contain even one independent clause, it is called a **sentence fragment**.

Choosing the best steps for **repairing** a sentence fragment depends on what type of fragment it is. If the fragment is a dependent clause, it can sometimes be fixed by simply removing a subordinating word, such as *when*, *because*, or *if*, from the beginning of the fragment. Alternatively, a dependent clause can be joined to a closely related neighboring sentence. If the fragment is missing some required part, like a subject or a verb, it may be fixed by simply adding the missing part.

Examples:

> **Fragment**: Because he wanted to sail the Mediterranean.
>
> **Removed subordinating word**: He wanted to sail the Mediterranean.
>
> **Combined with another sentence**: Because he wanted to sail the Mediterranean, he booked a Greek island cruise.

Example

Which of the following changes will NOT correct this sentence fragment?

Although she had found the coin first.

a. Remove *Although*.
b. Add a comma and she let her brother keep it after *first*.
c. Add *She let her brother keep the coin* before *although*.
d. Remove *first*.

Choice A suggests removing the word *although* to form the following sentence: She found the coin first. This option removes the subordinating conjunction to make the clause independent. The resulting sentence is complete, so removing *although* is an acceptable way to correct the fragment. Choice A is incorrect.

Choice B forms the following sentence: Although she had found the coin first, she let her brother keep it. A comma and an independent clause have been added to the sentence fragment to form a complex sentence. The resulting sentence is complete and written correctly, so choice B is incorrect.

Choice C forms the following sentence: She let her brother keep the coin although she had found the coin first. An independent clause has been added before the sentence fragment to form a complex sentence. This sentence is correctly written and complete, so choice C is an acceptable way to correct the fragment. Choice C is incorrect.

Choice D removes the word *first*, leaving *Although she had found the coin*. This is still a sentence fragment, since it is a single dependent clause. Choice D does not correct the fragment, so D is correct.

Run-on Sentences

Run-on sentences consist of multiple independent clauses that have not been joined together properly. Run-on sentences can be corrected in several different ways:

Join clauses properly: This can be done with a comma and coordinating conjunction, with a semicolon, or with a colon or dash if the second clause is explaining something in the first clause.

Example:

> **Incorrect**: I went on the trip, we visited lots of castles.
>
> **Corrected**: I went on the trip, and we visited lots of castles.

Split into separate sentences: This correction is best to use when the independent clauses are very long or when they are not closely related.

Example:

> **Incorrect**: The drive to New York takes ten hours, my uncle lives in Boston.
>
> **Corrected**: The drive to New York takes ten hours. My uncle lives in Boston.

Make one clause dependent: This is the easiest way to make the sentence correct and more interesting at the same time. It's often as simple as adding a subordinating word between the two clauses or before the first clause.

Example:

> **Incorrect**: I finally made it to the store and I bought some eggs.
>
> **Corrected**: When I finally made it to the store, I bought some eggs.

Reduce to one clause with a compound verb: If both clauses have the same subject, remove the subject from the second clause, and you now have just one clause with a compound verb.

Example:

> **Incorrect**: The drive to New York takes ten hours, it makes me very tired.
>
> **Corrected**: The drive to New York takes ten hours and makes me very tired.

Note: While these are the simplest ways to correct a run-on sentence, often the best way is to completely reorganize the thoughts in the sentence and rewrite it.

Comma Splices

A comma splice is a specific error that may appear in a run-on sentence. When a sentence has two independent clauses, but the clauses are joined with only a comma, a **comma splice** is formed. Remember that if two independent clauses are joined with a comma, a coordinating conjunction is also needed. Most of the solutions for fixing run-on sentences can also be used to correct a comma splice.

Example

Rick wants to go see a movie tomorrow he would miss his sister's recital.

Identify the change that would NOT correct this run-on sentence.

a. Add a comma after *tomorrow*.
b. Split it into two sentences between *tomorrow* and *he*.
c. Add a comma and *but* after *tomorrow*.
d. Add a subordinating conjunction to make one of the clauses dependent.

Choice A says to add a comma after *tomorrow*. This forms the following sentence: Rick wants to go see a movie tomorrow, he would miss his sister's recital. A comma has been used to join two independent clauses, but there is no coordinating conjunction. This choice forms a comma splice, so it is not an acceptable correction for this sentence. Choice A is the correct answer.

Choice B says to split the sentence into two sentences. This forms the following two sentences: Rick wants to go see a movie tomorrow. He would miss his sister's recital. Both of these sentences are complete. This is an acceptable way to correct the run-on sentence, so choice B is incorrect.

Choice C says to add a coordinating conjunction after *tomorrow*. This forms the following sentence: Rick wants to go see a movie tomorrow, but he would miss his sister's recital. A comma and a coordinating conjunction have been added between the two independent clauses. This is an acceptable way to correct a run-on sentence. Choice C is incorrect.

Choice D says to add a subordinating conjunction to make one of the sentences dependent. There are many new sentences that could be created by adding a subordinating conjunction. For example, consider the following sentence: Although Rick wants to go see a movie tomorrow, he would miss his sister's recital. Alternatively, the following sentence could also be created: Rick wants to go see a movie tomorrow even though he would miss his sister's recital. Both of these sentences have an independent clause and a dependent clause. These sentences are both complete and written correctly, so choice D is incorrect.

Example

Identify the sentence that has a comma splice.

a. Tom stopped at the store to buy supplies and his family met him at the campsite.
b. The ball rolled into the living room quietly, but it still startled the dog.
c. Theresa brought her mom some flowers, her mom did not have a vase.
d. Sweet potatoes, pecans, and brown sugar are all ingredients in my cousin's sweet potato casserole.

Choice A has two independent clauses joined by a coordinating conjunction. This is incorrect because there should be a comma before the coordinating conjunction. While the sentence is written incorrectly, there is no comma, so this sentence does not have a comma splice. Choice A is incorrect.

Choice B has two independent clauses joined by a comma and a coordinating conjunction. This is the correct way to write a compound sentence, so there is no error here. Choice B is incorrect.

Choice C has two independent clauses joined by a comma. This is incorrect because independent clauses should be joined together by a comma and a coordinating conjunction. When the comma is present without a coordinating conjunction between two independent clauses, a comma splice is formed. This means that choice C is correct.

Choice D is a simple sentence that contains one independent clause. The only commas used in this sentence are used to separate items in a list. There are no clauses that need to be joined or errors related to commas, so choice D does not contain a comma splice. Choice D is incorrect.

Parts of Speech

Nouns

When you talk about a person, place, thing, or idea, you are talking about a **noun**. The two main types of nouns are **common** and **proper** nouns.

Common Nouns

Common nouns are generic names for people, places, and things. Common nouns are not usually capitalized.

Examples of common nouns:

> *People*: boy, girl, worker, manager
>
> *Places*: school, bank, library, home
>
> *Things*: dog, cat, truck, car

Proper Nouns

Proper nouns name specific people, places, or things. All proper nouns are capitalized.

Examples of proper nouns:

> *People*: Abraham Lincoln, George Washington, Martin Luther King, Jr.
>
> *Places*: Los Angeles, California; New York; Asia
>
> *Things*: Statue of Liberty, Earth, Lincoln Memorial

Note: When referring to the planet that we live on, capitalize *Earth*. When referring to the dirt, rocks, or land, lowercase *earth*.

Singular and Plural Nouns

Singular nouns name **one** person, place, thing, or idea. **Plural nouns** name **more than one** person, place, thing, or idea. Most nouns have both a singular and plural form. Many plural nouns are spelled like the singular noun with an *-s* at the end, but this is not true for all plural nouns. Singular nouns that already end in an *s*, *o*, *ch*, *sh*, or *x* usually end in *-es* when they are in the plural form. Singular nouns that end in a consonant followed by the letter *y* will usually lose the *y* and end in *-ies* in the plural form, and words that end with the letter *f* or *fe* will usually lose the *f* and end in *-ves*.

Some plural nouns have much different spellings than their singular form, and some plural nouns are spelled the same as their singular form. There are more rules for spelling plural nouns, but these are the most common spelling changes.

Examples of singular nouns:

Typical nouns: dog, pencil, girl, store, hope, stingray

Nouns ending in *s*, *o*, *ch*, *sh*, or *x*: mass, hero, lunch, polish, fox

Nouns ending in a consonant and *y*: puppy, baby, fairy, sky

Nouns ending in *f* or *fe*: self, life, calf, hoof

Examples of plural nouns:

Typical nouns: dogs, pencils, girls, stores, hopes, stingrays

Nouns ending in *s*, *o*, *ch*, *sh*, or *x*: masses, heroes, lunches, polishes, foxes

Nouns ending in a consonant and *y*: puppies, babies, fairies, skies

Nouns ending in a vowel and *f* or *fe*: selves, lives, calves, hooves

COLLECTIVE NOUNS

Collective nouns are the names for a group of people, places, or things that function like singular nouns. The following are examples of collective nouns: *class, company, dozen, group, herd, team,* and *public*. Collective nouns usually require an article, such as *a*, *an*, and *the*, which shows that the noun is a single unit. For example, a choir is a group of singers. Even though there are many singers in a choir, the word choir describes a single group. If we refer to the members of the group, and not the group itself, it is no longer a collective noun.

Incorrect: The *choir are* going to compete nationally this year.

Correct: The *choir is* going to compete nationally this year.

Incorrect: The *members* of the choir *is* competing nationally this year.

Correct: The *members* of the choir *are* competing nationally this year.

EXAMPLE

Find the error in the following sentence.

Mary, Claudia, and Rachel each have two pet bunnys.

a. *Mary*, *Claudia*, and *Rachel* should all be common nouns.
b. *Bunnys* should be spelled *bunny*.
c. The subject should be *the three girls* instead of *Mary, Claudia, and Rachel*.
d. *Bunnys* should be spelled *bunnies*.

Before looking at all of the answer choices, first look at the sentence and try to find the error. The sentence has correct subject-verb agreement, and it is a complete sentence. The error is in the last word, *bunnys*. Remember that singular nouns ending in *y* are spelled differently when they are made plural. The *y* goes away and is replaced with *ies*, meaning that the plural of *bunny* is *bunnies*.

Choice A says that *Mary, Claudia, and Rachel* should really be *mary, claudia, and rachel*. This is incorrect, since *Mary*, *Claudia*, and *Rachel* are all proper nouns. Remember, proper nouns should always be capitalized. Choice A is incorrect.

Choice B says that *bunnys* should actually be the singular noun *bunny*. While *bunnys* is the error in the sentence, this solution is not correct because the sentence still has a plural object. There are six bunnies, not one bunny, so choice B is incorrect.

Choice C says the sentence should say *the three girls each have two pet bunnys*. This does not improve the sentence or resolve the spelling error at the end of the sentence. The error still remains, so choice C is incorrect.

Choice D says that *bunnys* should actually be spelled *bunnies*. This choice correctly points out the misspelling in the sentence and includes the correct spelling of the word. *Bunnies* is the correct plural form of *bunny*, so choice D is correct.

EXAMPLE

Which word or words in the following sentence should be capitalized?

My neighbor sent me a postcard from her trip to see the golden gate bridge.

a. Neighbor
b. Golden Gate Bridge
c. Sent
d. Postcard

Choice A says that *neighbor* should be capitalized. *Neighbor* is a common noun. It is not someone's name, a title, a place, or any other kind of proper noun. There is no reason for *neighbor* to be capitalized, so A is incorrect.

Choice B says that *golden gate bridge* should be capitalized. The Golden Gate Bridge is a famous bridge in California. From the sentence, it is also clear that the Golden Gate Bridge is a proper noun because the neighbor specifically went to see it, and it is an object with a title. *Golden Gate Bridge* is a proper noun, so B is correct.

Choice C says that *sent* should be capitalized. *Sent* is a verb. The only time a verb should be capitalized is when it is part of a title. In this sentence, *sent* is not part of a title and should not be capitalized. Choice C is incorrect.

Choice D says that *postcard* should be capitalized. *Postcard* is a common noun. In this sentence, it is not part of a name, title, or other proper noun. *Postcard* does not need to be capitalized in this sentence, so D is incorrect.

PRONOUNS

Pronouns are words that are used to stand in for nouns. There are several different types of pronouns, but the two main types are subjective and objective pronouns. **Subjective** nouns and pronouns that those that are the subject of a sentence. **Objective** nouns and pronouns are those that are an object in a sentence. Another important type of pronoun is the personal pronoun, which refers to people. Personal pronouns can be subjective or objective. **Possessive** nouns and pronouns show possession or ownership. Pronouns can also be singular or plural.

Singular

Subjective	Objective	Possessive
I	Me	My, Mine
You	You	Your, Yours
He	Him	His
She	Her	Her, hers
It	It	Its
Who	Whom	Whose

Plural

Subjective	Objective	Possessive
we	us	our, ours
you	you	your, yours
they	them	their, theirs

Reflexive: Reflexive pronouns are pronouns that function as the object of a sentence and refer to the subject. Examples of reflexive pronouns include *myself, yourself, himself, herself, itself, ourselves, yourselves*, and *themselves.*

Review Video: Nouns and Pronouns
Visit mometrix.com/academy and enter code: 312073

EXAMPLE

David accidentally scratched himself when he was fixing the broken vase.

What kind of pronoun is himself in the sentence above?

a. Reflexive
b. Subjective
c. Possessive
d. *Himself* is not a pronoun.

Choice A says that *himself* is a reflexive pronoun. Remember that reflexive pronouns are pronouns that refer to the subject after the subject has already been named in the sentence. In this sentence, *himself* refers to David, the subject of the sentence, to show that David is the one who was scratched. *Himself* does refer to the subject after the subject is named, so *himself* is a reflexive pronoun. Choice A is correct!

Choice B says that *himself* is a subjective pronoun. While *himself* refers to the subject, David, it is not the subject of the sentence. This means that *himself* is not a subjective pronoun, so choice B is incorrect.

Choice C says that *himself* is a possessive pronoun. Possessive pronouns are used to show who owns something. *Himself* is never used to show ownership. This means choice C is incorrect.

Choice D says that *himself* is not a pronoun at all. While reflexive pronouns may look different from other pronouns, since they are longer and usually end with *self* or *selves*, they are still pronouns that are used to represent nouns. *Himself* is a reflexive pronoun, so choice D is incorrect.

EXAMPLE

Which pronoun should go in the blank?

She gave her old rug to Thelma and ___.

a. I
b. We
c. Me
d. Our

In this sentence, there is a missing word. A good place to start when answering this question is to consider which part of the sentence is missing a word. Since this sentence only has one clause, a good place to start is with the subject, verb, and object. What is the verb? *Gave* is the verb, so the subject must be *she*, since she gave the old rug. This leaves the object. However, it looks like this sentence has a direct and indirect object. What is being given? Her old rug is being given, so it is the direct object. This means that the missing word is part of the indirect object.

The question says that the missing word is a pronoun. Not only is it a pronoun, but it must be an objective pronoun because it is part of the indirect object.

Choice A forms this sentence: She gave her old rug to Thelma and I. *I* is a subjective pronoun, meaning it should only be used in the subject of the sentence. The missing word must be an objective pronoun, so A is incorrect.

Choice B forms this sentence: She gave her old rug to Thelma and we. *We* is a plural and subjective pronoun. While the missing word could be singular or plural, it must be objective, so B is incorrect.

Choice C forms this sentence: She gave her old rug to Thelma and me. *Me* is an objective pronoun that completes the sentence. C is correct!

Choice D forms this sentence: She gave her old rug to Thelma and our. *Our* is a possessive pronoun. Since it also acts as an adjective, *our* also must be followed by a noun, so it cannot be the missing word. D is incorrect.

VERBS

If you want to write a sentence, then you need a verb. Without a verb, you have no sentence. The verb of a sentence indicates action or being. In other words, the verb shows something's action or state of being or the action that has been done to something.

Action Verbs and Linking Verbs

Action verbs show what the subject is doing. In other words, an action verb shows action. **Linking verbs** link the subject of a sentence to a noun or pronoun. They can also link a subject to an adjective, so the linking verb helps create a description. You always need a verb if you want a complete sentence. However, linking verbs on their own cannot be a complete sentence. Any verb that shows a condition and connects to a noun, pronoun, or adjective that describes the subject of a sentence is a linking verb.

Action: He sings. | Run! | Go! | I talk with him every day. | She reads.

Linking:

Incorrect: I am.

Correct: I am John. | The roses smell lovely. | I feel tired.

Review Video: Action Verbs and Linking Verbs
Visit mometrix.com/academy and enter code: 743142

Verb Tenses

A verb **tense** shows the different form of a verb to point to the time of an action. The present and past tense are indicated by the verb's form. An action in the present, *I talk,* can change form for the past: *I talked*. However, for future tense, an auxiliary, or helping, verb is sometimes needed to show the change in form. When writing a composition, it is important to use verb tenses consistently. Choose the best tense for the composition and do not switch to a different tense unless it is necessary or appropriate for a particular sentence or paragraph.

Present: I talk
Past: I talked
Future: I will talk

Present: The action happens at the current time.

Example: He *walks* to the store every morning.

Past: The action happened in the past.

Example: He *walked* to the store an hour ago.

Future: The action is going to happen later.

Example: I *will walk* to the store tomorrow.

Irregular Verbs

While most verbs gain the suffix -ed when used in the past tense, irregular verbs receive different spelling changes when they are written in the past tense. For example, *walk* is a regular verb, and it becomes *walked* when written in the past tense. However, *run* is an irregular verb because it becomes *ran* when written in the past tense.

Example

Which of the following words is a regular verb?

a. Run
b. Warn
c. Hold
d. Catch

Remember that regular verbs are verbs that end in *-ed* when they are written in the past tense. Irregular verbs are spelled differently in past tense.

Choice A says that *run* is a regular verb. What is the past tense of *run*? Is it *runned* or *ran*? The past tense of *run* is *ran*, so it is an irregular verb. Choice A is incorrect.

Choice B says that *warn* is a regular verb. The past tense of *warn* is *warned*, which means that *warned* is a regular verb Choice B is correct.

Choice C says that *hold* is a regular verb. What is the past tense of *hold*? Is it *holded* or *held*? The past tense of *hold* is *held*, so it is an irregular verb. Choice C is incorrect.

Choice D says that *catch* is a regular verb. What is the past tense of *catch*? Is it *catched* or *caught*? The past tense of *catch* is *caught*, so it is an irregular verb. Choice D is incorrect.

Adjectives

An **adjective** is a word that is used to modify a noun or pronoun. An adjective answers a question: *Which one? What kind?* or *How many?* Usually, adjectives come before the words that they modify, but they may also come after a linking verb.

> Which one? The *third* suit is my favorite.
>
> What kind? This suit is *navy blue.*
>
> How many? I am going to buy *four* pairs of socks to match the suit.

Comparison with Adjectives

Some adjectives are relative, and other adjectives are absolute. Adjectives that are **relative** can show the comparison between things. **Absolute** adjectives can also show comparison, but they do so in a different way. Let's say that you are reading two books. You think that one book is perfect, and the other book is not exactly perfect. It is not possible for one book to be more perfect than the other. Either you think that the book is perfect, or you think that the book is imperfect. In this case, perfect and imperfect are absolute adjectives.

Relative adjectives will show the different **degrees** of something or someone to something else or someone else. The three degrees of adjectives include positive, comparative, and superlative.

The **positive** degree is the normal form of an adjective.

Example: This work is *difficult.* | She is *smart.*

The **comparative** degree compares one person or thing to another person or thing.

Example: This work is *more difficult* than your work. | She is *smarter* than me.

The **superlative** degree compares more than two people or things.

Example: This is the *most difficult* work of my life. | She is the *smartest* lady in school.

Review Video: Adjectives
Visit mometrix.com/academy and enter code: 470154

EXAMPLE

What type of adjective is used in the following sentence?

The day John got married was the happiest day of his life.

a. Absolute
b. Comparative
c. Positive
d. Superlative

First find the adjective. The noun that is being described is *day*, so the adjective is *happiest.* Remember the difference between the different types of adjectives. Can one day be happier than another? How many days are being compared?

Choice A says *happiest* is an absolute adjective. Absolute adjectives cannot have different degrees. This sentence says that it was the happiest day of John's life, which means that it was happier than other days in his life. This means that *happiest* cannot be an absolute adjective, so A is incorrect.

Choice B says *happiest* is a comparative adjective. Comparative adjectives are used to compare two nouns. If John's wedding day is the happiest day of his life, then that day is being compared to thousands of other days. Also, *happiest* has the suffix *-est*, which is used in superlative adjectives that compare more than two nouns. These two facts show that *happiest* is not a comparative noun, so B is incorrect.

Choice C says that *happiest* is a positive adjective. Positive adjectives are the types of adjectives that simply describe nouns, but can be changed to either the comparative or superlative form. *Happy* is a positive noun because it can be used to describe a noun, but it can also be changed to *happier* or *happiest* in order to compare things. Since *happy* is a positive adjective that can be changed to *happiest* when more than two happy things are being compared, *happiest* is not a positive adjective. C is incorrect.

Choice D says that *happiest* is a superlative adjective. Superlative adjectives are used to compare three or more nouns. Since each of the thousands of days in John's life are being compared, it is true that more than three nouns are being compared. Again, the suffix *-est* is also used, which shows that this adjective is superlative. D is correct!

Example

Choose the word, or words, that best completes the sentence.

Marie's meeting was ____ than Dana's meeting.

a. The most boring
b. More boring
c. Boring
d. Bored

Choice A says that *the most boring* best completes the sentence. In the sentence, one meeting is being compared to another, so only two meetings are being compared. Since choice A uses the word *most*, this choice is a superlative adjective. Superlative adjectives are used to compare three or more nouns, not two. Choice A is incorrect.

Choice B says that *more boring* best completes the sentence. This choice uses the word *more*, instead of *most*. *More* is used in comparative adjectives to compare two nouns. Since two meetings are being compared in the sentence, the comparative adjective *more boring* is the best choice. B is correct.

Choice C says that *boring* best completes the sentence. The only word in this answer choice is *boring*, which is a positive adjective used to describe a noun. While the sentence suggests that both meetings were boring, the sentence is comparing the two meetings. Positive adjectives are used to describe, not compare, so choice C is incorrect.

Choice D says that *bored* best completes the sentence. Like choice C, *bored* is a positive adjective used to describe a noun. Since positive adjectives without words like *more* or *most* or suffixes like -*er* or -*est* are not used to compare, *bored* is not a good choice for this sentence. *Bored* is also used to describe a state or emotion, so it is not logical to describe a meeting as bored in this sentence. D is incorrect.

Adverbs

An **adverb** is a word that is used to **modify,** or describe, a verb, adjective, or another adverb. Usually, adverbs answer one of these questions: *When? Where? How?* and *Why?* The negatives *not* and *never* are considered adverbs. Adverbs that modify adjectives or other adverbs **strengthen** or **weaken** the words that they modify.

Examples:

He walks *quickly* through the crowd.

The water flows *smoothly* on the rocks.

Note: Adverbs are usually indicated by the suffix *-ly*, which has been added to the root word. For instance, *quick* can be made into an adverb by adding *-ly* to construct *quickly*. Some words that end in *-ly* do not follow this rule and can function as other parts of speech. Examples of adjectives ending in *-ly* include: *early, friendly, holy, lonely, silly*, and *ugly*. To know if a word that ends in *-ly* is an adjective or adverb, check your dictionary. Also, while many adverbs end in *-ly*, you need to remember that not all adverbs end in *-ly*.

Examples:

He is *never* angry.

You are *too* irresponsible to travel alone.

Types of Adverbs

Different types of adverbs are used to describe particular aspects of a verb, adjective, or other adverb. The following are examples of common types of adverbs:

Time: Some adverbs show when something was done, such as *yesterday*, *today*, or *in two days*.

Manner: Some adverbs show the way something was done, such as *hurriedly*, *neatly*, *grumpily*, or *loudly*.

Frequency: Some adverbs show how often something was done, such as *seldom*, *often*, *never*, or *often*.

Degree: Some adverbs show how much or to what degree something was done, such as *completely*, *barely*, *highly*, or *halfway*.

Comparison with Adverbs

The rules for comparing adverbs are the same as the rules for adjectives.

The **positive** degree is the standard form of an adverb.

Example: He arrives *soon*. | She speaks *softly* to her friends.

The **comparative** degree compares one person or thing to another person or thing.

Example: He arrives *sooner* than Sarah. | She speaks *more softly* than him.

The **superlative** degree compares more than two people or things.

Example: He arrives *soonest* of the group. | She speaks the *most softly* of any of her friends.

Review Video: Adverbs
Visit mometrix.com/academy and enter code: 713951

Example

Identify the adverb that shows frequency in the following sentence.

Sometimes I am so sleepy that I can barely keep my eyes open.

a. Barely
b. Sleepy
c. Sometimes
d. Open

This example says to find the adverb that shows frequency in the sentence. Remember that adverbs modify verbs or other adverbs, and there are different types of adverbs. With these facts in mind, can any of the answer choices be eliminated? Are any of these choices not adverbs?

Choices B and D are adjectives. In the sentence, *sleepy* describes the speaker, while *open* describes the speaker's eyes. Since these words describe nouns, they are not adverbs, so choices B and D can both be eliminated.

The question asks which adverb shows frequency. Choice A, *barely*, describes how well the speaker is able to keep his or her eyes open. Choice C, *sometimes*, describes how often the speaker feels very sleepy. Remember that frequency means how often something happens. This means that choice C is the correct answer, since *sometimes* shows how often the speaker feels this way.

PREPOSITIONS

A **preposition** is a word placed before a noun or pronoun that shows the relationship between an object and another word in the sentence.

Common prepositions:

<table>
<tr><td>about</td><td>before</td><td>during</td><td>on</td><td>under</td></tr>
<tr><td>after</td><td>beneath</td><td>for</td><td>over</td><td>until</td></tr>
<tr><td>against</td><td>between</td><td>from</td><td>past</td><td>up</td></tr>
<tr><td>among</td><td>beyond</td><td>in</td><td>through</td><td>with</td></tr>
<tr><td>around</td><td>by</td><td>of</td><td>to</td><td>within</td></tr>
<tr><td>at</td><td>down</td><td>off</td><td>toward</td><td>without</td></tr>
</table>

Examples:

> The napkin is *in* the drawer.
>
> The Earth rotates *around* the Sun.
>
> The needle is *beneath* the haystack.
>
> Can you find "me" *among* the words?

PREPOSITIONAL PHRASES

One important thing to know about prepositions is that they form special phrases, called prepositional phrases. A **prepositional phrase** begins with a preposition and ends with a noun or pronoun that is the object of the preposition. Normally, the prepositional phrase functions as an **adjective** or an **adverb** within the sentence.

Examples:

> The picnic is [on the blanket]

The picnic is on the blanket. (prepositional phrase: "on the blanket")

I am sick with a fever today. (prepositional phrase: "with a fever")

Among the many flowers, John found a four-leaf clover. (prepositional phrase: "Among the many flowers")

Review Video: Prepositions
Visit mometrix.com/academy and enter code: 946763

EXAMPLE

Which of the following could NOT complete the sentence?

She went ____ the cave.

a. Sadly
b. Into
c. From
d. Through

Choice A says that the missing word is *sadly*. The blank is between *went* and *the cave*, meaning that the missing word will connect these pieces of the sentence. While *sadly* could be used here to show how the girl felt, there would still be missing information. A preposition is needed here to show whether she entered, exited, or stood outside of the cave. *Sadly* is an adverb, so A is the correct answer.

Choice B says that *into* would complete the sentence. Does *into* complete the sentence without leaving missing information? To say *she went into the cave* is a logical, complete sentence. Choice B is incorrect.

Choice C says that the missing word is *from*. This creates the sentence *she went from the cave*. Since she could have left the cave to go somewhere else, this is also a logical, complete sentence. Choice C is incorrect.

Choice D says that *through* would complete the sentence. The sentence would read *she went through the cave*. Since she could have explored the whole cave or found an exit on the other side of it, *through* can logically complete the sentence. Choice D is incorrect.

EXAMPLE

Identify the prepositional phrase in the following sentence.

Mable visited the store to buy some vegetables.

a. To buy
b. Visited the store
c. The store to buy
d. To buy some vegetables

Remember the pieces of a prepositional phrase. Prepositional phrases should begin with a preposition and end with a noun or pronoun. Considering these rules, can any of the answer choices be eliminated? Choice B and choice C can be eliminated because neither choice begins with a preposition!

That leaves choices A and D. Choice A says that the prepositional phrase is *to buy*. This does start with a preposition, and it does give more information about Mable's trip to the store. However, it does not end with a noun or pronoun. Choice D says that the prepositional phrase is *to buy some vegetables*. Choice D begins with a preposition and ends with a noun, and it explains why Mabel went to the store.

Choice D is the only choice that has all of the pieces of a prepositional phrase, so D is correct!

CONJUNCTIONS

Conjunctions join words, phrases, or clauses and they show the connection between the joined pieces. **Coordinating conjunctions** connect equal parts of sentences. Coordinating conjunctions can also be used to create compound subjects and compound predicates, in addition to compound sentences. The **coordinating conjunctions** include: *and, but, yet, or, nor, for,* and *so.*

Compound Subjects:

> compound subject
>
> Terry *and* Marissa went to the movies last Saturday.
>
> compund subject
>
> Either pumpkin pie *or* apple pie would be a good dessert to bring to Thanksgiving dinner.
>
> compound subject
>
> Neither the clownfish *nor* the goldfish liked the new fish food very much.

Compound Predicates:

> compound predicate
>
> Veronica left school *and* picked up her sister from soccer practice.
>
> compound predicate
>
> The cat did not take a nap *or* play with the dog yesterday.

Compound Sentences:

> The rock was small, *but* it was heavy.
>
> She drove in the night, *and* he drove in the day.
>
> Bill dressed nicely today, *for* he must give an important presentation this afternoon.

EXAMPLE

Read the sentence below and answer the following question.

> Joseph went grocery shopping and put all of the groceries away when he got home.

In the sentence, the conjunction and helps create a compound...

a. Sentence
b. Subject
c. Predicate
d. Clause

In the sentence, where does the word *and* appear? Is it between two subjects, two verbs, or two independent clauses?

Find the subject of the sentence. Who did the actions in the sentence? Joseph did. While both *Joseph* and *he* are subjects in this sentence, they are not joined by *and* in this sentence, so the sentence does not contain a compound subject. Additionally, *Joseph* is the subject of an independent clause, while *he* is the subject of a dependent clause. Since this sentence contains a dependent clause, it is not a compound sentence. Choices A and B are incorrect.

Since *and* does not join two subjects or independent clauses, consider the verbs in the sentence, *went* and *put*. *And* is used in the sentence to show that Joseph did two actions. This information makes up the predicate, so the word *and* does help create a compound predicate. Choice C is correct.

While conjunctions can join clauses to form compound sentences, there is no such thing as a compound clause. Choice D is incorrect.

End Punctuation

Periods

Use a period to end all sentences except direct questions and exclamations. Periods are also used for abbreviations.

> Examples: 3 p.m. | 2 a.m. | Mr. Jones | Mrs. Stevens | Dr. Smith | Bill, Jr. | Pennsylvania Ave.

Note: An abbreviation is a shortened form of a word or phrase.

Question Marks

Question marks should be used following a **direct question**. A polite request can be followed by a period instead of a question mark.

> **Direct Question**: What is for lunch today? | How are you? | Why is that the answer?
>
> **Polite Requests**: Can you please send me the item tomorrow. | Will you please walk with me on the track.

Review Video: Question Marks
Visit mometrix.com/academy and enter code: 118471

Exclamation Marks

Exclamation marks are used after a word group or sentence that shows much feeling or has special importance. Exclamation marks should not be overused. They are saved for proper **exclamatory interjections**.

> Example: We're going to the finals! | You have a beautiful car! | "That's crazy!" she yelled.

Review Video: Exclamation Points
Visit mometrix.com/academy and enter code: 199367

Commas

The comma is a punctuation mark that can help you understand connections in a sentence. Not every sentence needs a comma. However, if a sentence needs a comma, you need to put it in the right place. A comma in the wrong place or a missing comma will make a sentence's meaning unclear. These are some of the rules for commas:

Use Case	Example
Before a **coordinating conjunction** joining independent clauses in compound sentences	Bob caught three fish, and I caught two fish.
Between **items in a series**	I will bring the turkey, the pie, and the coffee.
After **transition words**	Consequently, Joel's mother grounded him.

Review Video: When To Use a Comma
Visit mometrix.com/academy and enter code: 786797

Example

Choose the correct location for a comma in the following sentence.

Emily's dad reminded her five times to put her plate away but she still forgot.

a. After *away*
b. After *times*
c. After *but*
d. After *dad*

Remember that there are specific reasons for using commas in sentences. Are there any pieces of this sentence that look like they should be separated by a comma? There are not any lists, prepositional phrases, or transitions in this sentence. There are also not any phrases or dependent clauses. However, there are two independent clauses. Remember that independent clauses can be joined by conjunctions, and when they are joined by coordinating conjunctions, a comma is needed.

Look at the sentence and first identify the independent clauses. The sentence starts by saying that Emily's dad has reminded her to put her plate away. There is a subject, Emily's dad, and a predicate that gives information about his actions. Later in the sentence, Emily does an action, so she is the subject. This means that the first independent clause must be the information about Emily's dad. This clause ends just before the word *but* because Emily then becomes the subject. This means that *but* is the conjunction. Since it is a coordinating conjunction, this is a compound sentence.

Now consider the answer choices. Choices B and D can both be eliminated because they are not near the conjunction. This leaves A, after *away*, and C, after *but*. Commas are used just before coordinating conjunctions in compound sentences, so choice A is correct.

Quotation Marks

Use quotation marks to close off **direct quotations** of a person's written or spoken words, which are also called **dialogue**. Do not use quotation marks around indirect quotations. An indirect quotation gives someone's message without using the person's exact words. Use **single quotation marks** to close off a quotation inside a quotation.

> **Direct Quote**: Nancy said, "I am waiting for Henry to arrive."
>
> **Indirect Quote**: Henry said that he is going to be late to the meeting.
>
> **Quote inside a Quote**: The teacher asked, "Has everyone read Martin Luther King's 'I Have a Dream' speech?"

Quotation marks should be used around the titles of **short works**: newspaper and magazine articles, poems, short stories, songs, television episodes, and radio programs. Titles of **long works** should be italicized when they are part of a typed composition or underlined when they are part of a handwritten composition.

Examples:

> "Rip Van Winkle" (short story by Washington Irving)
>
> "O Captain! My Captain!" (poem by Walt Whitman)

Review Video: Quotation Marks
Visit mometrix.com/academy and enter code: 884918

Example

Identify the correct place for the first quotation mark in the following sentence.

> After her brother threw a baseball inside, Hallie said, If you ever do that again, I'll tell mom" and took the ball.

a. Before *Hallie*
b. Before *said*
c. Before *threw*
d. Before *if*

Remember that quotation marks are used to identify the words that someone wrote or said. This means that the correct place for quotation marks to go is around the words that were spoken aloud or written. This question asks where the quotation marks should start, which means that the answer will include the first word of dialogue. Consider this as you read each answer choice.

Choice A says the quotation marks should start before *Hallie*. Is *Hallie* the first word of dialogue? No, Hallie is the person saying the dialogue. The words *Hallie said* form the dialogue tag, which tells who said the dialogue and how they said it. Quotes do not include dialogue tags, so dialogue tags should not be inside of quotation marks. Choice A is incorrect.

Choice B says the quotation marks should start before *said*. The word *said* is also part of the dialogue tag. The dialogue tag should go right before the first quotation mark or right after the last one, but it should not be within the quotation marks. Choice B is incorrect.

Choice C says the quotation marks should start before *threw*. *Threw* is not part of the quotation, so it is certainly not the first word of dialogue. Choice C is incorrect.

Choice D says the quotation marks should start before *if*. In this sentence, *if* is the first word spoken by Hallie, which makes it the first word of dialogue. Remember that the first quotation mark should go right before the first word of the quote. This means that choice D is correct!

APOSTROPHES

An apostrophe is used to show **possession** or the **deletion of letters in contractions**. An apostrophe is not needed with the possessive pronouns *his, hers, its, ours, theirs, whose*, and *yours*.

APOSTROPHES SHOWING POSSESSION

Singular Nouns: David's car | a book's theme | my brother's board game

Plural Nouns that end with -*s*: the scissors' handle | boys' basketball

Plural Nouns that end without -*s*: Men's department | the people's adventure

Review Video: Apostrophes
Visit mometrix.com/academy and enter code: 213068

Review Video: Punctuation Errors in Possessive Pronouns
Visit mometrix.com/academy and enter code: 221438

APOSTROPHES IN CONTRACTIONS

Contractions are combinations of words. Contractions involve taking two words, removing at least one letter from one of the words, putting an apostrophe in its place, and removing the space. For example, *does not* can be written as the contraction *doesn't*. The *o* is removed from *not* and is replaced with an apostrophe, which represents the removed letter, so it appears as *n't*. The space after does is then removed, turning *does not* into the contraction *doesn't*. Some more examples of contractions are listed below.

First Word	Second Word	Contraction
Can	Not	Can't
Do	Not	Don't
She	Will	She'll
They	Will	They'll
He	Is	He's
It	Is	It's
They	Are	They're
I	Am	I'm

Not all words can be used to form contractions, but many small, commonly used words can.

EXAMPLE

Choose the correct possessive form of family in this sentence.

My familys Christmas card looks great this year!

a. Families'
b. Family's
c. Familys'
d. The word is already spelled correctly.

Before thinking about each choice, look closely at the sentence. The instructions say that the answer should be possessive. Since *family* is not a pronoun, the answer must have an apostrophe. Where should the apostrophe go? Recall the rules about apostrophes for singular nouns, plural nouns, and plural nouns ending in *s*.

Choice A says the correct spelling is *families'*. This word ends in *-ies*. Remember that when singular nouns ending in *y* are changed to the plural form, they are usually changed to end in *-ies*. Also, when plural possessive nouns end in *s*, the apostrophe goes after the *s*, and there is not another *s* added after it. Choice A is the correct plural possessive form of *family*. However, this is not the correct answer because the sentence is only talking about one family. A is incorrect.

Choice B says the correct spelling is *family's*. This is the singular possessive form of *family*. Unlike the sentence in the instructions, this choice has an apostrophe after the *y* in *familys*. The sentence is talking about the Christmas card belonging to one family, so this is the correct form. Choice B is correct.

Choice C says the correct spelling is *familys'*. This choice is not the correct singular possessive form or the correct plural possessive form of *family*. Choice C is incorrect.

Choice D says that *familys* is correct. This choice does not have an apostrophe. Remember that an apostrophe is needed for all possessive nouns and is only left out of possessive pronouns. Since *family* is not a pronoun, choice D is incorrect.

CAPITALIZATION

One important part of using correct grammar is properly capitalizing words. Usually, only nouns will be capitalized, but there are some exceptions. The most important capitalization rule is that the first word of every sentence, no matter what part of speech it is, should be capitalized. Another exception is that the pronoun *I* should always be capitalized.

Proper nouns are always capitalized, but sometimes it can be tricky to decide whether or not a noun is a proper noun. Some words that are usually common nouns may become proper nouns when used with other words or phrases. Also, when words that are not nouns are used with a noun, or when a group of words are used together as one noun, those words may also need to be capitalized.

TITLES OF PEOPLE

A title is a word that goes with a person's name and gives others information about them. These words are usually common nouns that are not capitalized alone, but when they are used with a person's name, they are capitalized. For example, the word *president* is not a proper noun, so it is not always capitalized. However, it should be capitalized when it is used with a person's name or in place of a person's name. For example, in the phrase *President George Washington*, the title is part of a person's name.

Holidays

Names of specific holidays should be capitalized. Holidays that are more general or, like birthdays and anniversaries, should not be capitalized. Words that can go with the names of specific holidays, like *day*, should also be capitalized when used in the name of a holiday.

Example:

My brother's birthday is the day after Christmas Day.

Geographic Names

Names of specific places, areas, and regions are proper nouns, so they should always be capitalized. The cardinal directions, north, south, east, and west, should be capitalized when they are part of the name of a specific place or area. However, cardinal directions should not be capitalized when used outside of the name of a place.

Titles of Books, Stories, and Essays

Most of the words in titles of things like books, stories, and essays should be capitalized, but some should not. The very first word in a title should always be capitalized. Any other word in a title that is a noun, pronoun, adjective, verb or adverb should be capitalized. Articles, such as *a* or *the*, should not be capitalized. Short conjunctions and prepositions are usually not capitalized.

The types of words and phrases in the chart below are proper nouns and should always be capitalized:

	Description	Example
Historical Periods	A range of time in history that is related to specific events or circumstances	During the Romantic Period, many authors and poets wrote about their emotions.
Historical Events	Names of important events that happened in history	Napoleon Bonaparte led France after the French Revolution.
Historical Documents	Titles of important papers or compositions that are connected to historical events	The Mayflower Compact was written to create rules and expectations for the colony in Plymouth.
Languages	Names of the different languages that people speak	I want to learn to speak Cantonese, Spanish, and German.
Races and Ethnicities	Words often used to describe a person's heritage or cultural group	Malia taught her granddaughter how to hula so she could share a tradition of her Native Hawaiian heritage with her.
Nationalities	Words that describe which country a person is from	My teacher who moved to Canada last year is Romanian.

Review Video: Capitalization in Grammar
Visit mometrix.com/academy and enter code: 369678

EXAMPLE

Identify the capitalization error in the sentences below.

> Some of the men who signed the Declaration of independence were Irish, Welsh, Scottish, and English. The document was signed near the beginning of the Revolutionary Period.

a. *Independence* should be capitalized.
b. *English* should be lowercase.
c. *Document* should be capitalized.
d. *Period* should be lowercase.

Choice A says that *independence* should be capitalized. The Declaration of Independence is a historical document, and *independence* is part of the document's title. That means that *independence* should be capitalized in the sentence, so choice A is correct.

Choice B says that *English* should be lowercase. *English* is always capitalized because it is a nationality and the name of a language. In this sentence, it shows that at least one of the men was born in England. *English* is correctly capitalized in this sentence, so choice B is incorrect.

Choice C says that *document* should be capitalized. While *document* refers to the Declaration of Independence in this sentence, it is not a proper noun. This means that *document* should stay lowercase, and choice C is incorrect.

Choice D says that *period* should not be capitalized. In this sentence, the word *period* is part of the phrase *Revolutionary Period*. This is the title of a historical period, so it follows the same rules as other titles. In names of historical periods, words like *period* and *era* should be capitalized. Choice D is incorrect.

EXAMPLE

Choose the word that should NOT be capitalized in the following title

> The Dragon Who Lived in A Barn

a. The
b. Who
c. Lived
d. A

Remember that when capitalizing titles, it is important to consider each word's part of speech. Nouns, pronouns, verbs, adjectives, and adverbs are always capitalized in titles. Which part of speech is each answer choice? Choice A is an article, choice B is a pronoun, choice C is a verb, and choice D is an article. This means that choice B and choice C can both be eliminated, since both of these words are correctly capitalized.

Choices A and D are both articles, and both are capitalized in the title. However, only one of them is correctly capitalized. Remember that the first word in a title should also be capitalized, no matter what part of speech it is. In this title, *the* is the first word, so it should be capitalized. Choice D, *a*, is an article and is not the first word in the title. Choice D is the correct answer.

Chapter Quiz

1. Every sentence always has a subject and a/an:

a. Imperative
b. Preposition
c. Predicate
d. Modifier

2. Which of the following sentences does NOT have an implied subject?

a. Take John on a quick walk.
b. Don't get lost.
c. John knows the way to the park.
d. Bring me back some flowers.

3. Which pronoun can be either singular or plural depending on what it is representing in the context of the sentence?

a. Nobody
b. Either
c. Several
d. All

4. Which of the following is written in third person perspective?

a. I am walking
b. He is walking
c. You are walking
d. We are walking

5. Which of the following best describes the function of an indirect object?

a. Shows how an action had an influence
b. Takes or receives the action of a verb
c. Explains or describes the subject
d. Shows that there is more information needed

6. Which of the following is a group of words that contains both a subject and a verb, and can be either independent or dependent?

a. Antecedent
b. Fragment
c. Phrase
d. Clause

7. What method of correcting run-on sentences is the easiest way to make the sentence correct and more interesting at the same time?

a. Split into separate sentences
b. Join clauses properly
c. Reduce to one clause with a compound verb
d. Make one clause dependent

8. Which of the following is a word placed before a noun or pronoun that shows the relationship between an object and another word in the sentence?

a. Adjective
b. Adverb
c. Preposition
d. Conjunction

9. Which of the following should be put in single quotation marks?

a. Quote inside a quote
b. Indirect quote
c. Direct quote
d. All of the above

Chapter Quiz Answer Key

1. C: See section **Predicates**

2. C: See section **Subjects**

3. D: See section **Depend on Context**

4. B: See section **Person Agreement Examples**

5. A: See section **Indirect Objects**

6. D: See section **Clauses**

7. D: See section **Run-on Sentences**

8. C: See section **Prepositions**

9. A: See section **Quotation Marks**

Written Essay

Essays

Essays usually focus on one topic, subject, or goal. There are several types of essays, including informative, persuasive, and narrative. An essay's structure and formality depend on the type of essay and its goal. While narrative essays typically do not include outside sources, other types of essays often require some research and the use of primary and secondary sources.

The basic format of an essay typically has three major parts: the introduction, the body, and the conclusion. The body is further divided into the writer's main points. Most essays will have at least three main points, but essays that go into more depth can have almost any number of main points.

An essay's introduction should answer three questions:

1. What is the **subject** of the essay?

   If an essay is about a book, the answer would include the title and author of the book, as well as any additional information needed, such as the subject or argument of the book.

2. How does the essay **discuss** the subject?

To answer this, the writer briefly summarizes the main points and the evidence supporting them to let readers know how the essay is organized and what information they can expect to read.

3. What will the essay **prove**?

   This information is in the thesis statement, usually the opening paragraph's last sentence, which clearly states the writer's message.

Using Sources in Essays

Sometimes writers use information from others in their work. This is most common in expository and persuasive writing. For an expository essay, a writer may not know all of the information that he or she needs to finish the composition. The writer may use other people's work to find the missing information and complete the composition. Persuasive writers may do research to find facts or statements from others that support their own beliefs and make their writing more persuasive. In both cases, research helps the writer find information that **supports** his or her **original work**.

Outside information must be relevant, true, and helpful to be appropriate for a composition. Writers must also be careful not to use too much outside information, since this can make the composition unoriginal. If a writer does use outside information, it is extremely important that the writer mention in the composition where the information came from. If the writer forgets or chooses not to say where the information came from, he or she has stolen someone else's work and presented it as their own. Doing this is called **plagiarism**.

Informational Texts

Informational texts, also called instructional or expository texts, are compositions written to inform the reader about a specific topic. An informational essay can inform readers in a variety of ways, such as giving them instructions, telling them facts about the topic, or teaching them why something happens. Informational texts should be logical, meaning that they should present information in an order that the reader can easily understand, and they should include the right amount of information so the writer successfully informs his or her audience of new information.

Informational texts should also focus on a **controlling idea**. In the introduction of an informational text, there may be a sentence or two that clearly state the essay's controlling idea. This sentence, or sentences, is called a **thesis statement**. The controlling idea should be clear throughout the composition. By emphasizing the controlling idea in the introduction, body, and conclusion, the writer can ensure that the controlling idea is clear. One way to make sure that the controlling idea is emphasized is to think about the purpose of each part of the essay. The introduction prepares the reader by telling them what the rest of the essay is about, so the controlling idea should be **introduced** in this section. The body tells the reader the information the writer wants to tell the audience, so this **explains** the controlling idea and facts about it to the reader. The conclusion is used to **remind** the reader of how the information in the body is related and **restates** the controlling idea one final time.

Review Video: Informational Text
Visit mometrix.com/academy and enter code: 924964

Structures or Organizational Patterns in Informational Texts

Informational text can be **descriptive**, meaning that it gives information that can be experienced through the five senses, or it answers the questions what, who, when, where, and why. One common method of organizing informational text is to put it in a certain sequence, or order. **Chronological** texts include events in the order that they occurred, from start to finish. **How-to**, or **instructional**, texts organize information into a series of instructions in the order in which the steps should be followed. **Comparison-contrast** structures of informational text describe different ideas to their readers by pointing out how things or ideas are similar and how they are different. **Cause and effect** structures of informational text describe events that occurred and the causes or reasons for those events. **Problem and solution** structures of informational texts introduce and describe problems and offer one or more solutions for each problem described.

Argumentative Writing

In argumentative writing, the writer expresses a belief or opinion that he or she wants to lead readers to agree with. When writing an argumentative composition, the writer should first identify the **topic** his or her opinion is about. The topic may be serious or fun, as long as there is one clear topic in the composition. The next step is for the writer to determine his or her opinion on the topic and determine why he or she holds that opinion. In order to persuade others to agree with their opinion, the writer must be able to give readers reasons to support the opinion. If the writer does not know why he or she has an opinion, it will be difficult to convince readers to agree. In addition to having reasons that support their opinion, writers should prepare examples that support each of these reasons in order to strengthen their composition.

Once the writer has determined his or her topic, opinion, and reasons for having the opinion, he or she is ready to begin writing an argumentative essay. In the introduction, the writer should capture the reader's interest, introduce the topic, and reveal his or her opinion about the topic. In the body of the composition, the writer should remind the reader of the opinion and give his or her reasons for holding the opinion. If the writer has any examples, facts, or other information that supports his or her opinion or reasons for believing it, these should also be included in the body. Writers may also use a body paragraph to mention opposing opinions or beliefs and explain why they disagree with them. As in other compositions, the conclusion should remind the reader of the essay's topic and purpose, as well as remind the reader how the opinion has been explained and supported. The conclusion should also invite the reader to continue thinking about the topic and writer's opinion. This can be done through questions or statements that lead readers to consider whether or not they agree with the author's opinion or what their own opinions are.

Review Video: Argumentative Writing
Visit mometrix.com/academy and enter code: 561544

Informative vs. Persuasive Writing

Informative writing, also called explanatory or expository writing, is written to show that something is true or factual, while **persuasive** writing is written to lead the reader to agree with something that may or may not be true or factual. While persuasive text is written to **persuade** readers to agree with the author's position, informative text simply **provides information** to readers. Informative writing **informs** readers about why or how something is as it is. This can include offering new information, explaining how a process works, or describing a concept for readers.

Facts and Opinions

Writers and readers must always be aware of the difference between fact and opinion. A **fact** can be tested and proven to be true. An **opinion**, on the other hand, is someone's personal thoughts or feelings. Opinions are often not changed by information. If an author writes that a newborn elephant is about five times taller than a newborn giraffe, then he or she is stating a fact. If the author writes that giraffes are more interesting than elephants, then he or she is giving an opinion because this cannot be proven to be true or false. Opinions are often supported by facts. For instance, the author might use a comparison between the way that giraffes eat and the way elephants eat as evidence of how giraffes are more interesting. An opinion supported by facts tends to be more convincing. On the other hand, when authors support their opinions with other opinions, readers should seriously think about and read the argument carefully to see whether it is logical and trustworthy.

Review Video: Distinguishing Fact and Opinion
Visit mometrix.com/academy and enter code: 870899

Responding to a Text

An essay prompt may require writers to write about a text they have read. When writing an essay like this, writers should show that they understand the text they have read. They may mention their own thoughts, ideas, and opinions in the essay. However, the main idea of the essay should be about the text mentioned in the prompt.

When planning the essay, writers should consider what the text is about and how it is written. Writers should identify the purpose, main idea, and structure of the text. For informational and persuasive texts, they should also think about the supporting details the author used in the text. All of these facts about the text will help writers understand the text well and allow the writer to create a response to the text.

Responding to Multiple Texts

Essay prompts may ask writers to write about more than one text. In this case, writers should identify the purpose, main idea, and structure of each text. They should also look at the kinds of supporting details that the author of each text uses. Once writers know these details, they should think about the differences and similarities between the texts. The main ideas of each text may oppose each other, or one may support the other. Writers will need to write about both texts in the essay, so they must understand both texts and the connection between the texts.

Chapter Quiz

1. What type of essay does NOT typically include outside sources?

a. Expository
b. Informative
c. Persuasive
d. Narrative

2. Which of the following is NOT true of informational texts?

a. Informational texts are also called instructional or expository texts
b. Informational texts should be logical
c. Informational texts should focus on a central idea
d. Informational texts can only be structured chronologically

3. In an argumentative essay, which of the following should be included in the body?

a. A reminder of the writer's opinion and his or her reasons for holding the opinion
b. Examples, facts, or other information that supports the writer's opinion
c. Opposing opinions or beliefs and explanations of why the writer disagrees with them
d. All of the above

Chapter Quiz Answer Key

1. D: See section **Essays**

2. D: See section **Structures or Organizational Patterns in Informational Texts**

3. D: See section **Argumentative Writing**

Informational Text Example

Below is a prompt for an informational text. There is also an example of an essay that addresses the prompt. There are multiple drafts of this essay to show what kinds of changes a writer may make during the writing process to improve his or her work.

Prompt:

In school, students learn about many subjects. Write about your favorite subject and explain why it is important to people's lives outside of school.

Rough Draft

Do you think math is boring? Well, think again! Solving math problems is so fun because they are like riddles made of numbers! Houses, computers, and even rocket ships would not exist without math! Math is my favorite subject and it is important.

Math is important because our houses would look very different without it. Next time you go home, look at the outside of your house. How many different shapes do you see? Before people lived in houses, they lived in shelters like caves and tents. Math helped people learn how to make buildings like houses, apartments, and hotels, so now we can live inside! People who build houses need math so that they know what shape the house should be and how big or small each part should be.

Computers have made our lives easier, since it is possible to find almost any information in seconds! Computers also make it easier for people to communicate with each other. Phones and TVs use computers, but we also need math to use them! The only person I can think of who doesn't use a phone, TV, or computer is my baby brother. Computers use very complicated math problems, so many types of math are very important for computers to work!

The third reason math is important is that it helps people invent things like rocket ships so we can visit space. Math is used to build the rockets, make the rockets fly, and help the astronauts travel through space! Rocket ships don't affect our daily lives right now, but they can help scientists continue to invent things that could change our lives in the future. Who knows, math could help us reach Mars and find a way to live there!

As you can see from these examples, math is important because it affects our daily lives and makes it possible for us to achieve new things and think of new possibilities. If you thought math was boring before, I bet you don't think it is now!

Revised Draft

Do you think math is boring? Well, think again! Solving math problems is so fun because they are like riddles made of numbers! Houses, computers, and ~~even rocket ships~~ would not exist without math! Math is my favorite subject and it is important because it helps people complete very important jobs that affect others' daily lives.

Math is important because our houses would look very different without it. Next time you go home, look at the outside of your house. How many different shapes do you see? Before people lived in houses, they lived in shelters like caves and tents. Math helped people learn how to make buildings like houses, apartments, and hotels, so now we can live inside! People who build houses need math so that they know what shape the house should be and how big or small each part should be.

Computers have made our lives easier, since it is possible to find almost any information in seconds! Computers also make it easier for people to communicate with each other. Phones and TVs use computers, but we also need math to use them! The only person I can think of who doesn't use a phone, TV, or computer is my baby brother. Computers use very complicated math problems, so many types of math are very important for computers to work!

~~The third reason math is important is that it helps people invent things like rocket ships so we can visit space. Math is used to build the rockets, make the rockets fly, and help the astronauts travel through space! Rocket ships don't affect our daily lives right now, but they can help scientists continue to invent things that could change our lives in the future. Who knows, math could help us reach Mars and find a way to live there!~~

As you can see from these examples, math is important because it affects our daily lives and makes it possible for us to achieve new things and think of ~~new possibilities~~. Math affects where we live and how we communicate and find information. If you thought math was boring before, I bet you don't think it is now!

Revised Draft Notes

Remember the purpose of the revising stage of the writing process. When revising, it is important to look at the whole composition. Do all of the paragraphs strengthen the composition? Do the introduction and conclusion help the reader understand the controlling idea and main points?

First, look at the underlined words. These are words that have been added in the revision process. In the introduction, a clause has been added to the last sentence. This clause strengthens the composition by giving more information about the essay's controlling idea. Now this sentence, the thesis, tells the reader not only what the writer's favorite subject is, but also why the writer thinks it is important to others' lives. A sentence has been added to the conclusion, as well. This sentence strengthens the conclusion by emphasizing why the writer thinks math is important. The sentence makes the conclusion more interesting and reminds the reader of the writer's main points.

Next, look at what has been crossed out in this essay. Some words in the introduction and conclusion have been removed, and a whole paragraph has been omitted! Why is that? There were no huge errors, and the writing made sense, but those details and facts did not support the controlling idea very well. When the writer added to the introduction, he or she made the controlling idea clearer. However, the controlling idea says that math is important because it affects people's daily lives. While rocket science is important, it is not important for daily life. The writer made a smart choice to remove this information and should later replace it with more relevant information about how math impacts daily life.

Edited Draft

Do you think math is boring? Well, think again! ~~Solving math problems is so fun because they are like riddles made of numbers!~~ Houses, computers, and ~~even rocket ships~~ would not exist without math! Math is my favorite subject and it is important.

Math is important because our houses would look very different without it. Next time you go home, look at the outside of your house. How many different shapes do you see? People who build houses need math so that they know what shape the house should be and how big or small each part should be. Before people lived in houses, they lived in shelters like caves and tents. Math helped people learn how to make buildings like houses, apartments, and hotels, so now we can live inside!

Another reason math is important is because it makes inventions like computers possible. Computers have made our lives easier, since it is possible to find almost any information in seconds! Computers also make it easier for people to communicate with each other. For example, devices like phones and TVs use computers, but we also need math to use them! ~~The only person I can think of who doesn't use a phone, TV, or computer is my baby brother.~~ Computers use very complicated math problems, so many types of math are very important for computers to work!

~~The third reason math is important is that it helps people invent things like rocket ships so we can visit space. Math is used to build the rockets, make the rockets fly, and help the astronauts travel through space! Rocket ships don't affect our daily lives right now, but they can help scientists continue to invent things that could change our lives in the future. Who knows, math could help us reach Mars and find a way to live there!~~

As you can see from these examples, math is important because it affects our daily lives and makes it possible for us to achieve new things and think of ~~new possibilities~~. If you thought math was boring before, I bet you don't think it is now!

Edited Draft Notes

Since the writer has revised his or her work, the next step is to edit the composition. Remember that editing is very similar to revising, but editing usually includes paying attention to each paragraph, instead of the whole composition. Look at the changes that were made to each paragraph.

In the introduction, the second sentence was removed. Why was it removed? It was a good sentence, and it gave information about math! While it was engaging and it mentioned math, it was still off topic. The prompt asks why math is important for people's lives. This sentence tells why math is enjoyable to learn about, so it does not prepare the reader for the information in the rest of the essay. Also, the introduction already has a hook, so this sentence does not help the paragraph or the composition.

What has been changed in the second paragraph? The underlined sentence was in the rough draft, but it was in a different part of the paragraph. This paragraph is about how math has affected the buildings people live in. In the rough draft, the underlined sentence was at the end! This sentence supports the paragraph, but it was not very helpful or logical at the end of the paragraph. The writer moved it in the editing step of the writing process. Now this paragraph makes more sense and its sentences are in a logical order that helps the reader understand the writer's point.

There are a few changes in the second paragraph. A sentence was added to the beginning of the paragraph. Before, the paragraph simply started by explaining that computers are convenient inventions. The new sentence is helpful because it creates a transition and tells the reader what the main point of the paragraph is. The next difference is the added words at the beginning of the fourth paragraph. These words also form a transition, and they show the reader that the sentence contains examples that support the main point of the paragraph. Finally, a sentence has been removed from this paragraph. This sentence may be related to the information in the paragraph, but it does not strengthen it or support the main point.

The remaining marks are left to remind the writer that the information about rockets and math still need to be replaced. This information will be added before the final draft is finished.

FINAL DRAFT

Do you think math is boring? Well, think again! Houses, computers, and even cars would not exist without math! Math is my favorite subject, and it is important because it helps people complete very important jobs that affect others' daily lives.

Math is important because our houses would look very different without it. Next time you go home, look at the outside of your house. How many different shapes do you see? People who build houses need math so that they know what shape the house should be and how big or small each part should be. Before people lived in houses, they lived in shelters like caves and tents. Math helped people learn how to make buildings like houses, apartments, and hotels, so now we can live inside!

Another reason math is important is because it makes inventions like computers possible. Computers have made our lives easier, since it is possible to find almost any information in seconds! Computers also make it easier for people to communicate with each other. For example, devices like phones and TVs use computers, so we also need math to use them! Computers use very complicated math problems, so many types of math are very important for computers to work!

The third reason math is important is that it helps people invent things like cars so we can travel fast. Math is used to build cars and make them drive. Cars are very important because they help us go places quickly when we are in a hurry or have an emergency. Before cars, people used wagons, horses, and trains to get around. Can you imagine how long it would take to go on vacation if you had to ride a horse? Cars are helpful and convenient, and we would not have them without math!

As you can see from these examples, math is important because it affects our daily lives and makes it possible for us to achieve new things. Math affects where we live, how we communicate and find information, and how we travel. If you thought math was boring before, I bet you don't think it is now!

Final Draft Notes

This is the final draft! In this draft, information has been added to the introduction and conclusion, and there is a new paragraph. Notice that these additions have replaced all of the information about rockets that was removed in the revising step. Now, the essay discusses how math has helped people create houses, computers, and cars. Cars impact more people's daily lives than rockets do, so these additions help strengthen the composition by supporting the controlling idea, or thesis. The additions in the introduction and conclusion make it easier for the reader to understand the writer's main points and read the composition.

Evaluation

The essay answers the prompt and is on topic throughout the composition. The controlling idea is clear and is stated in the introduction, supported in the body, and restated in the conclusion. The thesis statement restates parts of the prompt and gives the reader a preview of the rest of the essay. The body uses well-structured paragraphs to explain the supporting details and examples and connects them to the controlling idea. The conclusion also emphasizes the controlling idea and supporting details and invites the reader to consider what they have read.

The essay is also interesting and written with a variety of sentence types. It uses transitions and good paragraph structure to make the essay easy for the reader to understand. The introduction also uses a hook to get the reader's attention and help him or her relate to the information in the essay. The examples are all things that most readers will be able to see in their own lives. Not only does this essay answer the prompt and have appropriate structure, but it also makes use of good, engaging, and relatable details.

Reading Practice Test #1

Questions 1–12 pertain to the following story:

<u>The Tournament</u>

(1) The sun was warm as Keith and Joe walked home from school.

(2) "Tomorrow will be a perfect day to skateboard," Keith said. "Let's meet at the park at ten o'clock."

(3) "I can't," Joe said. "I have a karate tournament. I've been doing it since I was six."

(4) "Can't you get out of it?" Keith complained. "This will be the first sunny Saturday of spring."

(5) "I have a better idea. Come with me to the tournament." said Joe.

(6) "It sounds boring," Keith said.

(7) "It won't be boring," Joe promised. "Will you come?"

(8) "I'll ask my mom," Keith said.

(9) Later, Keith called Joe. "Mom said I can go. When will we meet?"

(10) "We'll pick you up at nine o'clock," Joe said. "See you tomorrow!"

(11) On the drive to the tournament, Joe told Keith that karate was a tradition in his family. Joe's father started studying karate when he was six, just like Joe. His grandfather learned karate as a boy in Okinawa.

(12) "Where's Okinawa?" Keith asked.

(13) "It's an island off the tip of Japan," Joe told him. "That's where my grandfather grew up."

(14) "Is your grandfather your karate teacher?" Keith asked.

(15) Joe laughed. "No. He's too old to teach anymore. I study with Master Lee in a dojo downtown."

(16) Joe explained that a dojo was a karate school. Master Lee taught many students in his dojo. In the tournament, Joe would compete against friends from his dojo and students from other dojos. He was nervous and excited.

(17) When they arrived at the tournament, Master Lee met them near the door. Joe introduced Keith to Master Lee. Master Lee smiled and bowed to Keith. Keith bowed back, even though he felt a little funny.

(18) Master Lee led them into the arena. The wide floor was divided into several rings. In each ring, students competed. Around the rings, family and friends cheered and offered encouragement. Joe waved to friends from his dojo.

(19) "I have to get dressed," Joe told Keith. "I'll be back in a few minutes."

(20) Joe disappeared into a locker room. When he came back, he wore a white top and pants. A green belt was tied around his waist.

(21) Keith grinned. "Nice outfit. Why is your belt green? It seems like everyone here has a different color of belt."

(22) Joe explained that belt color showed the skill level of a student. Beginners had white belts. After passing some tests, they earned a yellow belt. Then they earned a green belt. That was the skill level Joe had achieved. His next step was to earn a brown belt. Someday Joe hoped to earn a black belt like his father and grandfather and Master Lee. Then he could teach karate to others.

(23) Master Lee called Joe to a nearby ring. It was almost time for Joe to compete. He did some stretching exercises to prepare his body for competition. When Joe's name was called, he bowed to Master Lee and walked to the center of the ring.

(24) Keith felt worried. "What if he gets hurt?" Keith asked Joe's dad.

(25) Joe's dad explained it was a light contact competition. Students made only gentle, controlled contact with each other. They were judged on speed and accuracy rather than force or power. Keith was relieved.

(26) As the match began, Keith cheered for Joe as he punched, kicked, and blocked against his opponent's attacks. Joe was really good at karate! Keith's and Joe's dads yelled and clapped as the match came to an end.

(27) Joe was breathless when he came to stand beside them. They waited anxiously for the judges' decision. The four judges conferred quietly at their table. Finally, they announced their decision: all four points went to Joe. Joe won the match!

(28) As the tournament continued, Joe kept winning matches. Keith cheered louder and louder with every win. He felt proud that someone as talented as Joe was his friend. He also admired the way his friend used his karate skills to honor his family's heritage. Keith hoped he could attend another tournament with Joe very soon!

1. In what season is the story set?

a. Spring
b. Summer
c. Fall
d. Winter

2. What is a dojo?

a. A karate technique
b. A karate school
c. A karate teacher
d. A karate student

3. In paragraph 27, what is the definition of the word "conferred"?

a. Argued
b. Joked
c. Decided
d. Discussed

4. Based on the story, why does Joe want Keith to come to the karate tournament with him?

a. Joe wants Keith to understand that karate is important to him
b. Joe does not want Keith to go skateboarding without him
c. Joe wants Keith to meet Master Lee and Joe's dad
d. Joe wants Keith to be jealous of his karate skills

5. Which of the following best describes how Keith's attitude toward the karate tournament changes between paragraph 6 and paragraph 28?

a. Keith's attitude does not change at all
b. Keith goes from thinking the tournament is boring to hoping to attend another one
b. Keith goes from thinking that karate is an awesome sport to thinking that karate is boring
d. Keith decides he doesn't want to skateboard anymore; he wants to study karate

6. Complete the following chart based on information in the story:

White belt
Yellow belt
____
Brown belt
Black belt

a. Blue belt
b. Green belt
c. Red belt
d. Purple belt

7. Part A: What is the primary purpose of this story?

a. To show how important karate is to Joe
b. To show how much Keith likes skateboarding
c. To show how long Keith and Joe have been friends
d. To show what a good teacher Master Lee is

Part B: Which sentence or sentences from the story supports your answer from Part A?

a. Joe introduced Keith to Master Lee.
b. "I can't," Joe said. "I have a karate tournament. I've been doing it since I was six."
c. "Tomorrow will be a perfect day to skateboard," Keith said.
d. Keith hoped he could attend another tournament with Joe very soon!

8. Based on the information given in the story, how likely is Joe to keep practicing karate?

a. Very unlikely
b. Somewhat unlikely
c. Somewhat likely
d. Very likely

9. Part A: Which of the following statements about the story is a fact?

a. By the end of the story, Keith wants to take karate
b. Because Joe wins all his matches, Master Lee is obviously an excellent teacher
c. Joe's father and grandfather both practice karate
d. None of the other students in Master Lee's dojo are as good as Joe

Part B: Which sentence or sentences from the story supports your answer from Part A?

a. Joe kept winning matches.
b. He felt proud that someone as talented as Joe was his friend.
c. Finally, they announced their decision: all four points went to Joe. Joe won the match!
d. Joe's father started studying karate when he was six, just like Joe. His grandfather learned karate as a boy in Okinawa.

10. Based on the story, how does practicing karate honor Joe's family heritage?

a. Karate is taught in Okinawa, and Joe's grandfather is Okinawan
b. Karate is a tradition in Joe's family, practiced by three generations
c. Karate is popular in the town where Joe and his family live
d. Many Asians practice karate, and Joe is Asian

11. Which sentence is an accurate summary of the story?

a. Keith initially wants Joe to go skateboarding, but Joe has a karate tournament and invites Keith to watch. At the tournament, Keith gains a deeper appreciation and understanding of the sport, and he is very proud of Joe after he won.
b. Joe skips his karate tournament to go skateboarding with Keith, but he regrets his decision when he realizes how important the tournament was to his family.
c. Keith and Joe argue about whether skateboarding or karate is better, and their friendship is tested as they refuse to support each other's interests.
d. Keith wants Joe to go skateboarding, but Joe has a karate tournament and invites Keith to watch. Joe loses the karate tournament after Keith distracts him. This makes Joe question whether he should continue to practice karate at all.

12. What color belt is required to teach Karate?

a. Blue belt
b. Green belt
c. Black belt
d. Purple belt

Questions 13–19 pertain to the following passages:

Remember the Alamo

(1) In the early 1700s, the Spanish established missions throughout the land we now know as the state of Texas. One of the most famous of these missions was San Antonio de Valero, better known by its nickname: the Alamo. This was the most successful mission in the area, and it served a number of purposes for the surrounding communities.

(2) For over a century, the Alamo served as an active mission. Church services were held in the cool, shady buildings, providing welcome relief from the blazing summer sun. Couples were married at the Alamo. Babies were baptized there. The Alamo also served as a trading post, supply depot, and communication center. In later years, however, the Alamo served its most famous and—arguably—most important role; it was a fortress for freedom fighters.

(3) During the 1830s, Texas was in a battle for independence from Mexico, which owned it at that time. This struggle came to a head in 1836 when 184 Texans, led by William Travis, holed up in the Alamo. Travis and other famous American fighters—including Jim Bowie and Davy Crockett—fought side by side with farmers, ranchers, cowboys, and businessmen. Those brave men held off Mexican General Santa Anna's army for 13 days from the secure walls of the Alamo.

(4) Finally, in the gray, early morning light of March 6, 1836, General Santa Anna and an army of 4,000 soldiers overran the Alamo. Every man in the Alamo died that day, but their ability to hold out for nearly two weeks gave American General Sam Houston the time he needed to assemble a more substantial army. General Houston soon defeated General Santa Anna, and Texas won its independence, thanks in great part to the brave men who defended the Alamo and the cause of freedom.

13. What was the official name of the mission nicknamed "the Alamo"?

a. San Antonio de Valente
b. San Antonio de Verde
c. San Antonio de Valero
d. San Antonio de Vallejo

14. Which of the following represents the author's main purpose in writing this story?

a. To inform
b. To influence
c. To entertain
d. To persuade

15. What was the main motivation for the men who fought at the Alamo?

a. Wealth
b. Fame
c. Safety
d. Freedom

16. Based on the information in paragraph 2, what was the purpose of the Alamo?

a. It was designed as a war fortress
b. It was designed to serve many purposes in the community
c. It was designed as a trading post
d. It was designed as a saloon

17. Which of the following is a statement of opinion?

a. William Travis, Davy Crockett, and Jim Bowie fought at the Alamo
b. All the men who fought to defend the Alamo died in the battle
c. General Santa Anna was eventually defeated by General Sam Houston
d. General Santa Anna was a better leader than William Travis

18. How many Americans died while defending the Alamo?

a. 184
b. 13
c. 136
d. 47

19. Which of the following people participated in the battle of the Alamo? Select all that apply.

a. General Sam Houston
b. Davy Crockett
c. Jim Bowie
d. General Santa Anna
e. Andrew Jackson

Use the story "A Day at the Alamo" to answer questions 20–25:

A Day at the Alamo

(1) Just before spring break, Eric's class took a trip to visit the Alamo. Before they left, they read about William Travis, Jim Bowie, and Davy Crockett in their history books. They also read about General Santa Anna and his army. Eric couldn't wait to see the place where the actual battle for the Alamo occurred.

(2) Eric watched buildings roll by as the school bus drove into downtown San Antonio. Near the River Walk, the bus stopped and the class climbed out.

(3) "Stay together, please," Mrs. Morgan, Eric's teacher, directed the class. "After I check us in, we will go listen to a history talk."

(4) A few minutes later, Mrs. Morgan led the class to a patio area. A guide met them there and told the story of the Alamo, from its establishment by the Spanish to the famous standoff and battle in 1836. Eric listened carefully. He wanted to remember all the details to help him complete the History Hunt worksheet Mrs. Morgan had given them.

(5) When the history talk was over, Mrs. Morgan divided the class into small groups. Each group was assigned a parent volunteer and given an hour to complete a self-tour of the Alamo and the grounds. During that time, they were supposed to look for all the necessary answers to complete their History Hunt worksheets. In an hour, all groups would meet at the gift shop.

(6) Eric loved walking through the old buildings and viewing the artifacts. He liked the gardens and the Long Barrack Museum, but his favorite building was the Shrine. He especially liked the old bell that was kept in a small room in the Shrine. Eric could imagine Davy Crockett himself ringing that bell!

(7) Soon the hour was up, and Eric's group headed for the gift shop. While there, Eric used his allowance to buy a book about Davy Crockett and a small Texas flag. Back on the bus, Eric waved his flag proudly at passing cars. He knew he would always remember the Alamo.

20. Where does the story say the Alamo is located?

a. Just outside San Antonio
b. Near the San Antonio River
c. In downtown San Antonio
d. Across the river from San Antonio

21. Which artifact was Eric's favorite during his trip to the Alamo?

a. The Texas flag
b. The old bell
c. The Long Barrack Museum
d. The gardens

22. Complete the following schedule for Eric's class trip:

1. Arrive at the Alamo and check in
2. Attend history talk on the patio
3. Divide into groups for self-tour
4. ____________________

a. Meet in the gardens
b. Meet on the patio
c. Meet at the gift shop
d. Meet at the bus

23. Why was Eric so excited about visiting the Alamo?

a. He wanted to see where the battle occurred
b. He heard there were interesting items in the gift shop
c. He enjoyed riding on the school bus
d. His friends were excited about the trip

24. In paragraph 6, what is the best definition of the word "artifacts"?

a. Buildings
b. Historical items
c. Documents and pictures
d. Furnishings

25. Part A: Which paragraph tells the most about Eric's favorite experiences at the Alamo?

a. Paragraph 4
b. Paragraph 5
c. Paragraph 6
d. Paragraph 7

Part B: Which sentence supports your answer from Part A?

a. He especially liked the old bell that was kept in a small room in the Shrine.
b. When the history talk was over, Mrs. Morgan divided the class into small groups.
c. While there, Eric used his allowance to buy a book about Davy Crockett and a small Texas flag.
d. Eric listened carefully.

Use both "Remember the Alamo" and "A Day at the Alamo" to answer questions 26 and 27:

26. What theme is central to both of these stories, joining them together?

a. Love of freedom
b. Davy Crockett
d. Independence of Texas
d. History of the Alamo

27. Which of the following represents the biggest difference between the stories?

a. One involves a school class and the other doesn't
b. The Alamo changed a lot between the two stories
d. One is nonfiction and the other is fiction
d. One involves General Santa Anna and the other doesn't

Questions 28-40 pertain to the following passage:

A Lesson Learned

(1) Beautiful melodies floated from Uncle Eddie's guitar. Kari listened with wonder. The way Uncle Eddie made the guitar sing filled Kari with a desire to learn to play. She wanted to make beautiful music too.

(2) "Teach me to play, Uncle Eddie," Kari begged.

(3) Uncle Eddie looked intently at Kari. "Learning to play isn't easy, Kari. It takes hard work and practice. Are you ready for that?"

(4) "I am! I promise." Kari was thrilled. She was sure playing the guitar would come easily for her. "When can we start?"

(5) "I'll come by at two o'clock on Saturday," Uncle Eddie said. "Be ready to work hard."

(6) Kari laughed. "I will," she promised. "Thanks, Uncle Eddie. See you Saturday!"

(7) Kari could hardly wait for Saturday to come. She dreamed about the songs she would play. She imagined impressing her friends with her skills. Kari was sure she would be a guitar expert in no time. She was so excited.

(8) On Saturday afternoon, Uncle Eddie rang the doorbell. Kari ran to let him in.

(9) "Ready to learn?" Uncle Eddie greeted her.

(10) Kari nodded. She followed him into the family room. She waited for him to get out his guitar and teach her a song, but he didn't even open the case. Instead, he took a book from his music bag.

(11) "We'll start with a history of the guitar," Uncle Eddie said. "Did you know stringed instruments have been around for thousands of years?"

(12) Kari was unimpressed. "Wow," she said.

(13) Uncle Eddie said guitars came from Spain more than 500 years ago. He said they could be used to play a variety of music styles and were one of the most popular instruments.

(14) Kari sighed. "That's great, Uncle Eddie, but I just want to play. When can I start playing songs?"

(15) Uncle Eddie laughed. "Patience, Kari. There's a lot to learn about the guitar before you're ready to play one."

(16) "Like what?" Kari asked.

(17) Uncle Eddie handed her a diagram of a guitar. He explained the two basic guitar parts were the body and the neck. These were made up of other parts.

(18) "The tuning pegs are tightened and loosened so the strings make the right notes," Uncle Eddie told Kari.

(19) Then he showed her the nut at the top and the bridge at the bottom that held the strings in place. He pointed out the fingerboard all along the neck and the frets that helped with finger placement. Finally, he described the top of the body—the sounding board—with a hole in the middle to produce a sweet sound.

(20) Uncle Eddie told Kari to learn the names of the guitar parts as her homework for the next lesson.

(21) "But I don't want homework," Kari protested. "I want to play songs! I didn't even play one note."

(22) With a sigh, Uncle Eddie opened his guitar case and took out his instrument. He played a simple folk song. When he played the song three times, Kari grinned.

(23) "I've got it! I can do this," Kari insisted.

(24) Uncle Eddie showed her how to hold the guitar. Kari started to play, but the notes were all wrong. It didn't sound at all like Uncle Eddie's beautiful music. Kari handed the guitar back to Uncle Eddie with frustration.

(25) "Maybe the guitar isn't for me," she said.

(26) Without a word, Uncle Eddie took out a CD and put it in the player behind him. Tuneless, horrible music filled the room. Kari laughed.

(27) "Hey! That person is worse than I am," she said.

(28) Uncle Eddie smiled. "That's me at my first lesson."

(29) "No way!" Kari said.

(30) "Yep," said Uncle Eddie. "Kari, I've played for 15 years. It took time and practice to get this good."

(31) "Do you think I could play like you someday?" Kari asked.

(32) "If you work hard," answered Uncle Eddie.

(33) "Maybe I should start with my homework for our next lesson," Kari said.

(34) Uncle Eddie hugged her. "That sounds like a great place to start."

28. Based on the story, which of the following best qualifies Uncle Eddie to teach guitar lessons to Kari?

a. He is Kari's uncle
b. He has taught many guitar students before
c. He is looking for work
d. He knows how to play the guitar very well

29. Which part of the guitar is used to help strings make the right notes?

a. Tuning pegs
b. Fingerboard
c. Bridge
d. Soundboard

30. In paragraph 3, what does the word "intently" mean?

a. In a focused way
b. In a disinterested way
c. In a happy way
d. In a disgusted way

31. Which of the following belongs in the empty box according to the sequence of the story?

Kari wants to learn to play the guitar.	⇨	Uncle Eddie agrees to teach her.	⇨		⇨	Kari becomes bored and frustrated.	⇨	Kari learns it takes hard work to play guitar.

a. Kari plays well on her first try.
b. Uncle Eddie begins the lesson with the history and structure of the guitar.
c. Uncle Eddie does not show up for the lesson.
d. Kari's friends decide they want Uncle Eddie to teach them, too.

32. What is the main theme of this story?

a. To show that Uncle Eddie is not a good teacher
b. To show that Kari is not a good student
c. To show that learning to play the guitar is boring
d. To show that learning to play the guitar takes hard work

33. In what point of view is this story written?

a. First person
b. Second person
c. Third person
d. All of the above

34. What is the difference between Uncle Eddie's feelings and Kari's feelings about learning to play the guitar?

a. Uncle Eddie feels it will be hard, while Kari feels it will be easy
b. Kari feels it will be hard, while Uncle Eddie feels it will be easy
c. Both Kari and Uncle Eddie feel it will be hard
d. Both Kari and Uncle Eddie feel it will be easy

35. How does the author show in paragraph 14 that Kari is unhappy with Uncle Eddie's history lesson on guitars?

a. By saying, "Kari was unhappy."
b. By having Kari say something unkind to Uncle Eddie
c. By writing, "Kari sighed."
d. By having Kari leave the room

36. Who is playing the "horrible music" Kari hears in paragraph 26?

a. Uncle Eddie's first student
b. Uncle Eddie
c. Kari
d. Kari's father

37. Based on the information presented in the story, which of the following is a fact instead of an opinion?

a. Uncle Eddie has been playing guitar for 15 years
b. Kari will never learn to be a good guitar player
c. Playing the guitar is a boring hobby
d. Everyone who plays the guitar knows a lot about guitar history

38. As used in paragraph 19, what does the word "bridge" mean?

a. a passage way over something
b. a piece of wood that supports guitar strings
c. a way to play the guitar
d. a way to hold the guitar

39. Which of these is NOT a part of a guitar?

a. Fingerboard
b. Neck
c. Strapping
d. Frets

40. In what paragraph did it seem like Kari had given up on guitar?

a. paragraph 14
b. paragraph 25
c. paragraph 29
d. paragraph 31

Answers and Explanations for Reading Test #1

1. A: is the best choice because paragraph 4 indicates that the story is set in spring. B, C, and D are not the best choices because the story is set in spring.

2. B: is the best choice because paragraph 16 explains that a dojo is a karate school. A, C, and D are not the best choices because they present incorrect definitions of the word "dojo."

3. D: is the best choice because the correct definition of "conferred" is "discussed." A, B, and C are not the best choices because they are not proper definitions of "conferred."

4. A: is the best choice because Joe invites Keith to the tournament so that Keith will understand that karate is important to Joe. B and D are not the best choices because they do not accurately represent Joe's attitude in the story. C is not the best choice because it does not represent Joe's main motivation for inviting Keith to the tournament.

5. B: is the best choice because Keith's attitude changes from thinking karate is boring to hoping to attend another tournament. A is not the best choice because Keith's attitude does change throughout the story. C and D are not the best choices because they do not accurately represent the change in Keith's attitude.

6. B: is the best choice because a "green belt" properly completes the sequence. A, C, and D are not the best choices because they are not standard karate belt colors and cannot complete the presented sequence.

7. Part A: A: is the best choice because the primary purpose of the story is to show that karate is important to Joe. C is a good answer, but it is not the best choice because it does not reflect the primary purpose of the story. B and D are not the best choices because they do not represent themes or purposes from the story.

Part B: B: This sentence shows how committed Joe is to Karate and it shows that it is important enough to him to not skip his tournament.

8. D: is the best choice because karate is very important to Joe, so he is very likely to keep practicing it. A, B, and C are not the best choices because they do not accurately represent Joe's likelihood of continuing to practice karate.

9. Part A: C: is the best choice because it is a fact that Joe's father and grandfather both practice karate. A, B, and D are not the best choices because they are all statements of opinion instead of fact.

Part B: D: This sentence supports the fact that Joe's father and grandfather both practice karate.

10. B: is the best choice because karate is part of Joe's family heritage, as three generations of his family practice karate. A and D are good answers, but they are not the best choices because they do not demonstrate how Joe's family heritage involves karate. C is not the best choice because it does not express how karate honors Joe's family heritage.

11. A: A summary is a short overview of the story. Joe invited Keith to come to his Karate tournament. At first Keith thought it would be boring and did not want to go, but once he was there he loved it. He liked learning about the sport and watching his friend compete. In the end he even decided he would like to go again.

12. C: In the story Joe says that he hopes he can reach a black belt so that he can teach karate one day.

13. C: is the best choice because the official name of the Alamo is San Antonio de Valero. A, B, and D are not the best choices because they list incorrect official names for the Alamo.

14. A: is the best choice because the author's purpose in writing "Remember the Alamo" is clearly to inform. B, C, and D are not the best choices because they represent inaccurate purposes for the story.

15. D: is the best choice because freedom was the main motivation for those who fought at the Alamo. A, B, and C are not the best choices because they do not portray the primary motivation for the Alamo fighters.

16. B: is the best choice because the Alamo was designed to serve many purposes in the community. A, C, and D are not the best choices because they do not reflect the real purpose behind the design of the Alamo.

17. D: is the best choice because it is a statement of opinion. A, B, and C are not the best choices because they are all statements of fact.

18. A: is the best choice because 184 Americans died defending the Alamo. B, C, and D are not the best choices because they are inaccurate answers.

19. B, C, D: Jim Bowie, Davy Crockett, and General Santa Anna were all at the Battle of the Alamo. General Sam Houston fought General Santa Anna's army later, and Andrew Jackson was president at that time.

20. C: is the best choice because the story states that the Alamo is located in downtown San Antonio. A, B, and D are not the best choices because they name incorrect locations for the Alamo.

21. B: is the best choice because according to paragraph 6, the old bell is Eric's favorite artifact. A, C, and D are not the best choices because none of those things are Eric's favorite artifact.

22. C: is the best answer because it accurately completes the schedule for Eric's class trip. A, B, and D are not the best choices because they do not properly represent the events of the class trip.

23. A: is the best choice because the story says Eric was excited to see where the battle occurred. B, C, and D are not the best choices because they reflect inaccurate motivations for Eric's excitement.

24. B: is the best choice because the best definition for the word "artifacts" is "historical items". A, C, and D are not the best choices because they are incorrect definitions.

25. Part A: C: is the best choice because paragraph 6 describes Eric's favorite experiences at the Alamo. A, B, and D are not the best choices because those paragraphs do not describe Eric's favorite experiences.

Part B: A: This sentence comes from paragraph 6 and talks about one of Eric's favorite experiences.

26. D: is the best choice because the two stories both have a central theme of the history of the Alamo, linking them together. While A, B, and C are mentioned in both stories, they are not the best choices because they do not represent central themes in the stories.

27. C: is the best choice because the biggest difference between the two stories is that one is nonfiction and the other is fiction. While A, B, and D all represent differences between the stories, they are not the best choices because those differences are not as fundamental as the difference between nonfiction and fiction.

28. D: is the best choice: Uncle Eddie is qualified to teach guitar because he plays very well. A, B, and C are not the best choices because they do not represent Uncle Eddie's best qualification to teach guitar.

29. A: is the best choice because the tuning pegs of a guitar are used to help the strings make the right note. B, C, and D are not the best choices because they are not used to help tune the guitar.

30. A: is the best choice because "intently" means "in a focused way." B, C, and D are not the best choices because they do not represent accurate definitions of "intently."

31. B: is the best choice because it best completes the sequence of the story. A, C, and D are not the best choices because they do not complete the sequence according to the progression of the story.

32. D: is the best choice because the main theme of the story is to show that learning to play the guitar takes hard work. A, B, and C are not the best choices because they do not represent the main theme of the story.

33. C: is the best choice because this story is written in third person. A, B, and D are not the best choices because they represent incorrect points of view for this story.

34. A: is the best choice because Uncle Eddie feels playing the guitar will be hard, but Kari feels it will be easy. B, C, and D are not the best choices because they represent inaccurate perspectives for Uncle Eddie and Kari according to the story.

35. C: is the best choice because paragraph 14 says "Kari sighed" as the author's way of indicating Kari's displeasure. A, B, and D are not the best choices because they do not reference details included in paragraph 14.

36. B: is the best choice because Uncle Eddie is playing the "horrible music" Kari hears in paragraph 26. A, C, and D are not the best choices because they do not represent the correct person who is playing the "horrible music."

37. A: is the best choice because it is the only statement of fact from the story. B, C, and D are not the best choices because they are all statements of opinion instead of fact.

38 B: In paragraph 19, the word "bridge" is used to describe the piece of wood that holds the guitar strings.

39. C: There are several parts of the guitar mentioned in the story. Body, neck, tuning pegs, strings, bridge, fingerboard, frets, and the sounding board are all parts of a guitar. A strapping is not a part of a guitar.

40. B: In paragraph 25, Kari says "Maybe the guitar isn't for me," This sounds like she has given up.

Language Practice Test #1

Questions 1–4 pertain to the following passage:

Amazing Pandas

(1) When a baby panda is born, it is about the size of a breakfast sausage. (2) Tiny and almost furless, it snuggles close to its mother. (3) The baby panda stays very near its mother for the first two months of life. (4) Until it is two months old, the panda's eyes cannot open. (5) It relies on its mother for everything.

(6) Even when they are open, a baby panda still needs its mother to give it food. (7) Baby pandas nurse up to eight times a day until they are 18 months old. (8) During this time, baby pandas also chew on bamboo, but this is just for fun. (9) They are not strong enough to eat the bamboo.

(10) Bamboo does not have many vitamins or calories, though, so pandas must spend up to 14 hours a day eating just to stay full! (11) Sometime between 12 and 18 months of age, pandas begin eating bamboo. (12) Even though they can eat without help from their mothers, the pandas still do not wander far from home. (13) Pandas stay with their mothers until they are fully grown.

(14) A fully grown panda is about five feet long and weighs about 200 pounds. (15) They live in the forests of China, although many now live in zoos and other places. (16) In fact, there are fewer than 2,000 pandas left in the wild because their habitats have been destroyed to build cities. (17) People need to care for pandas so these amazing animals will always be with us.

1. Which of the following sentences can be added before sentence 1 to show the central idea of the passage?

a. Pandas are interesting and valuable members of the animal kingdom.
b. You can tell that pandas are mammals because they have fur and are warm-blooded.
c. You don't have to travel far to see a panda because many zoos have pandas.
d. While my favorite animals are all small, large animals like pandas are also interesting.

2. The word *they* in sentence 6 is unclear. Choose the phrase that should be used instead of *they* in sentence 6.

Even when ___________ are open, a baby panda still needs its mother to give it food.

its eyes
its teeth
its arms
its friends

3. Which sentence should be added after sentence 7 to provide a supporting detail?

a. Baby pandas look around a lot during this stage, since they could not open their eyes before.
b. Baby pandas also start learning how to walk when they are this age.
c. Mother pandas are fully grown, so they can eat bamboo when they are hungry.
d. All of this food gives baby pandas the nutrients they need to keep growing.

4. Which sentence is the best choice for the first sentence of paragraph 3?

a. Sentence 10
b. Sentence 11
c. Sentence 12
d. Sentence 13

Questions 5–8 pertain to the following passage:

The Bubblegum Blunder

(1) My favorite type of candy is bubblegum. (2) I could chew it every day! (3) For my birthday this year, my grandparents gave me a whole bag of bubblegum pieces. (4) I was so excited to have bubblegum any time I wanted.

(5) The next afternoon, I was getting ready to watch television after lunch. (6) Since I had just finished my meal, I got a piece of bubblegum. (7) I laid on the couch and chewed my bubblegum as I watched a show. (8) It was the perfect afternoon! (9) I realized that I had lost my bubblegum! (10) I sat up right away to find it so I could throw it away. (11) It wasn't on the pillow, it wasn't on the couch cushion, and it wasn't even on the floor!

(12) I went off to find my mom and tell her what had happened. (13) But, when she saw me, she let out a loud gasp. (14) "June," she exclaimed, "you have a piece of bubblegum in your hair!"

(15) "Oh, that's where it went!" I said. (16) I tried to take the gum out of my hair, but it didn't come out!

(17) "It won't come out that way," my mom explained.

(18) I teared up and asked, "Will we have to cut it out of my hair?"

(19) "Maybe not," she said. (20) "Come with me to the kitchen. (21) I bet we can get it out a different way."

(22) We went to the kitchen, and I was shocked to see my mom get ice from the freezer in the kitchen. (23) "How will that help?" I asked.

(24) "It will make the gum harden. (25) Hopefully, that will make it less sticky, so it will come out more easily." (26) She held the ice against the gum, and after a few minutes, it happened. (27) However, she was only able to get some of the gum out. (28) "Alright, that worked a little bit, but I think we need to try something else."

(29) I was shocked again when she got the peanut butter out of the pantry. (30) "Won't peanut butter make an even bigger mess?" I shrieked.

(31) She laughed and answered, "It will be pretty messy, but it will help. (32) Since peanut butter has oil in it, it will also help make the gum less sticky." (33) She took out a small glob of peanut butter and put it on the gum that was still in my hair. (34) We let it sit there for a few minutes, and, while we waited, my mom told me to

be more careful when chewing bubblegum. (35) "I don't think we'll need to cut it out this time, but it could be worse if it happens again," she said.

(36) She spent a few minutes working with the peanut butter, and she finally got all of the gum out. (37) "Thank you!" I said. (38) "I'm so glad we didn't have to cut it out of my hair!"

(39) "Me too!" she said. (40) "Just remember to pay more attention next time!"

5. A sentence should be added at the end of paragraph 1 to improve the introduction. Which sentence would be best to add after sentence 4?

a. The bag included different flavors of gum, like grape, apple, lemon, and regular.
b. My parents told me I could only have two pieces each day, but that was alright with me.
c. I started planning out all the times I would chew my bubblegum.
d. But, little did I know, I had an important lesson to learn about my favorite candy.

6. Which of the following sentences should be inserted after sentence 8 to add a supporting detail?

a. I had chosen the regular flavor of bubblegum.
b. I was having a great time, until disaster struck.
c. I had even had my favorite sandwich for lunch.
d. I snuggled up in a new blanket I had gotten for my birthday.

7. What is the best revision of sentence 22?

a. We went to the kitchen, and I was shocked to see my mom get ice from the freezer.
b. We went to the kitchen, I was shocked to see my mom get ice from the freezer in the kitchen.
c. We went to the kitchen and I was shocked to see my mom get ice from the freezer in the kitchen.
d. We went to the kitchen shocked to see my mom get ice from the freezer in the kitchen.

8. The phrase *it happened* in sentence 26 is unclear and should be replaced. Which of the following phrases should be used to replace this phrase?

a. the gum came out
b. the gum got stickier
c. the gum hardened
d. her hands got cold

Questions 9–12 pertain to the following passage:

Bats: Our Flying Friends

(1) Most people are afraid of bats because bats have sharp teeth and only come out at night. (2) People worry that bats will bite them but bats do not feed on people. (3) Most bats in North America eat insects that they catch in the air with their teeth. (4) Some bats eat mice, birds, frogs, lizards, and other bats. (5) One kind of bat in Mexico catches fish in the claws of its hind legs. (6) In Asia, large bats called flying foxes eat fruit. (7) Other bats with long noses drink sweeter juice from flowers.

(8) All bats are mammuls, and they are the only ones that fly. (9) Bats live everywhere in the world except Antarctica and the North Pole. (10) Most bats do not drink blood. (11) Only vampire bats drink blood. (12) Vampire bats live in Central and South America. (13) They land on animals and bite them to make a tiny cut. (14) Then they lap up the blood with their tongues. (15) Vampire bats always bite people. (16) If they do bite, they do not take much blood. (17) However, bats may carry germs that cause disease.

9. Which change would correct the mistake in sentence 2?

a. Change *worry* to *worries.*
b. Change *bite* to *bit.*
c. Add a comma after *them.*
d. Change *on* to *with.*

10. Which change would correct the mistake in sentence 7?

a. Change *bats* to *bat.*
b. Change *drink* to *drank.*
c. Change *sweeter* to *sweet.*
d. Change *flowers* to *flower's.*

11. Which change needs to be made to sentence 8?

a. Change *are* to *were.*
b. Change *mammuls* to *mammals.*
c. Change *fly* to *flies.*
d. This sentence does not need to be changed.

12. Which change needs to be made to sentence 15?

a. Add a comma after *bats.*
b. Change *always* to *rarely.*
c. Change *bite* to *bites.*
d. Change *people* to *persons.*

Questions 13–16 pertain to the following passage:

The Science of Music

(1) Nearly every song on the radio has sounds from a stringed instrument in it. (2) Weather the instrument is a violin or an electric guitar, the sounds of plucked, strummed, or bowed strings are essential to today's music. (3) You know the recognizable sound of these instruments, but did you know that the reasons they can be heard is that they cause vibrations in the air? (4) Every time a musician plays one of these instruments, he or she moves the string. (5) The string then vibrates, which moves the air around the string and sends a sound wave through the air. (6) These sound waves travel through the air, and cause vibrations within a person's ears. (7) The ears work with the brains so that the person can understand the note that was played. (8) Different ways of playing an instrument produce different types of sound waves, and those waves allow us to experience a variety of musicul sounds.

13. Which change would correct the mistake in sentence 2?

a. Change Weather to Whether.
b. Change instrument to instruments.
c. Change electric to Electric.
d. Change strings to string's.

14. Which change would correct the mistake in sentence 3?

a. Change *sound* to *sownd.*
b. Change *reasons* to *reason.*
c. Change *they* to *them.*
d. Change *in* to *by.*

15. Which change would correct the mistake in sentence 6?

a. Change *These* to *This.*
b. Change *travel* to *will travel.*
c. Remove the comma after *air.*
d. Change *person's* to *persons.*

16. Which change would correct the mistake in sentence 8?

a. Change *playing* to *played.*
b. Remove the comma after *waves.*
c. Change *us* to *we.*
d. Change *musicul* to *musical.*

Questions 17–20 pertain to the following passage:

Paper Perfect

(1) Do you use a lot of paper? (2) Do you just throw it away when you are done with it? (3) If you want to avoid throwing away paper, there are plenty of ways to achieve this. (4) You may have heard the phrase "reduce, reuse, and recycle" when talking about items like used paper. (5) Reducing and recycling are great ways to avoid throwing things in the trash, but they are not always possible to do. (6) However, with a little creativity, you can find plenty of ways to reuse paper at home.

(7) One easy way to reuse paper is to turn it into art. (8) When you are getting ready to paint, think about any thick paper you have that you might throw away. (9) Instead of buying new paper or a canvas, you can paint directly on old paper, so you don't have to buy paper. (10) The paper can be the canvas for art, or it can become art itself! (11) Mosaics are works of art that are made from pieces of glass or stone. (12) Colorful paper from old magazines, newspapers, or flyers can be ripped up to make these pieces. (13) These pieces can be glued to a surface, such as old paper or cardboard, to create a picture and reuse paper.

(14) Another way to reuse paper is to turn it into new paper. (15) To do this, first rip or cut the paper into small pieces. (16) Next, ask an adult to blend the paper pieces with water to create a pulp. (17) Then, mix the pulp with more water in a large container. (18) Ask an adult to help you scoop up a layer of pulp using a wire screen. (19) Then, lay the layer of pulp on something that will absorb the water and keep the layer flat. (20) Let it sit, then use a towel to press more water out of the layer. (21) Once the layer is dry, you will have a new sheet of paper!

(22) You can also reuse paper by folding it. (23) Origami is a popular activity that involves folding paper to make fun, three-dimensional objects, like animal figurines. (24) You can use old paper and origami techniques to make small decorations. (25) Supplies, like folders and bookmarks, and tools, like small boxes or drawer dividers, can also be made from folded paper. (26) Sometimes, to make sure the object is sturdy, you may need to reinforce the paper by gluing multiple pieces together. (27) If you do use glue, consider ways that you can reuse the glue container!

(28) Next time you have paper to throw away, consider these options. (29) Reusing paper can help create less trash and save money, and it is easy to do! (30) Used paper can be more than another piece of trash. (31) It may be the solution to a problem—or your next piece of artwork!

17. Sentence 9 repeats information. Which part of sentence 9 should be removed to correct this error?

a. Instead of buying new paper
b. or a canvas, you can paint
c. directly on old paper
d. so you don' t have to buy paper

18. There is information missing in paragraph 2. Which of the following sentences should be added after sentence 11?

a. Making a mosaic is a great way to recycle glass instead of paper.
b. But you can make a paper mosaic by using tiny pieces of paper instead of glass or stone.
c. Artists have been making mosaics for centuries.
d. Mosaics use irregular shapes, so they have a unique look to them.

19. Sentence 22 is missing information. Which of the following phrases should be added to the end of sentence 22?

a. into a paper airplane
b. before you throw it away
c. to create small objects
d. until it is very small and thick

20. Sentence 27 is not the best concluding sentence for paragraph 4. Which of the following sentences would be a better concluding sentence for that paragraph?

a. With practice, you can learn to make all kinds of paper objects for different purposes.
b. Multiple sheets of paper glued together are sturdier than one sheet of paper.
c. You can also make your own glue at home instead of buying it.
d. Though you can make many of things from paper, not everything can be made from paper.

Questions 21–24 pertain to the following passage:

Polar Bears

(1) Polar bears are fascinating creatures. (2) Did you know that they are among the biggest bears in the world? It's true! They're even bigger than grizzly bears. (3) A male polar bear can weigh anywhere from 800 to 1500 pounds and can grow to be betwean eight and ten feet long. (4) Polar bears spent much of their time in or on the water. (5) In fact, their scientific name is Ursus maritimus, which is Latin for "bear of the sea. (6) While they are born on land and do spend a lot of time on land, they spend much of their time in the water or on ice formations because their main food source is seals.

(7) Polar bears are only found in areas around the North Pole, and in only five countries: Norway, Canada, Russia, Greenland, and the United States (only in Alaska). (8) Their fur is white, which helps them blend in with the snow. (9) This makes it easier to sneak up on seals and catch them, because it's hard for the seals to see them. (10) They also have long snouts and long necks. (11) These allow polar bears to look down into holes in the ice over the sea so they can catch seals underwater. (12) Their thick fur allows them to live in areas with very cold temperatures, their strong claws and teeth are ideal for catching and eating their food. (13) They also have very wide feet. (14) Their big feet or claws allow them to walk on ice without slipping.

21. Which change would correct the mistake in sentence 3?

a. Change *can* to *could.*
b. Change *from* to *with.*
c. Change *betwean* to *between.*
d. Add a comma after *eight.*

22. Which change would correct the mistake in sentence 4?

a. Change *bears* to *bear.*
b. Change *spent* to *spend.*
c. Change *their* to *there.*
d. This sentence does not need to be changed.

23. Choose the conjunction that should be added after the comma in sentence 12.

Their thick fur allows them to live in an area with very cold temperatures,_____ their strong claws and teeth are ideal for catching and eating their food.

or
and
so
nor

24. Which change needs to be made to sentence 14?

a. Change *or* to *and.*
b. Change *allow* to *allowed.*
c. Change *without* to *with out.*
d. Change *slipping* to *sliping.*

Questions 25–28 pertain to the following passage:

Gabby Douglas: Star of the Olympics

(1) She stands at the chalk bowl, whitening her hands, her determined face staring at the uneven bars. She moves to the bars, salutes the judges, and mounts. Over the next few minutes, she performs an almost perfect routine, hailed by some experts as one of the most amazing performances by anyone at the 2012 Olympic Games. She moves through each maneuver of the routine with the confidence of a mature competitor, while the watching world holds its collective breath. As she sticks her dismount, she flashes that beautiful, contagious smile, and we jump out of our seats, cheering. She's done it again!

(2) Gabby, born on December 31, 1995, in Virginia Beach, Virginia, began her formal gymnastics training at the age of 6 years old. By the time she was 8 years old, she had won a state championship. So, when Gabby turned 14, she left her hometown and family to move to West Des Moines, Iowa, to train with Liang Chow. Chow is a trainer known all over the world for turning American gymnasts into Olympic champions and gold medalists. Travis and Missy Parton, who have a daughter who is also a student of Chow's, offered to be Gabby's host family. Gabby very quickly became close to the Parton family and even considers herself to be a "big sister" to the Parton's four daughters.

(3) Leaving her home and family was difficult for Douglas but soon proved to be a strategic move. In 2010, at the Nastia Liuken SuperGirl Cup, Gabby made her debut on the national level, winning fourth all-around. She continued to compete throughout the rest of 2010, winning fifth all-around at the 2010 Pan American Championships, earning her a place on the US team. In 2011, the US team won the gold medal in the team finals at the World Artistic Gymnastics Championships in Tokyo, Japan. When she won the 2012 Olympic Trials in San Jose, California, Gabby

earned a place on the US national team that would represent the United States at the 2012 Summer Olympics in London.

(4) Gabby Douglas arrived at the 2012 Olympic Games in London, England, as an underdog, but she left the competition as not only a world champion, but also America's sweetheart. The 4'11", 16-year-old young lady mesmerized the world with her power, flexibility, and form. Many who were familiar with her career were concerned that Gabby would crack emotionally under the great pressure of participating in the world's most prestigious athletic event, but her nerves appeared to be made of steel. Even in the most intense moments of the competition, Gabby seemed focused and calm, ready to help Team America bring home the gold. Not only is she the first African American female to win gold in the individual all-around event, but she has also been nicknamed "Flying Squirrel" because of the way she seems to fly through the air when competing on the bars.

(5) During the London Olympics, Gabby stood out as a star, not only for her gymnastic skills, but also for her fun personality and support of the other members of the US team. Since the Olympics, she has received much attention from the media, and she has appeared on the cover of several magazines, such as Sports Illustrated and Time. In 2012, she was named Sportswoman of the Year by the Women's Sports Foundation. She has received several endorsement deals with companies such as Kellogg's and Procter & Gamble.

(6) For Gabby, it's all been about a dream. "I think when you have a dream, you won't let anyone stop you," she said. And her dream has definitely come true.

25. Which of the following sentences is a compound sentence?

a. Leaving her home and family was difficult for Douglas but soon proved to be a strategic move.
b. Since the Olympics, she has received much attention from the media, and she has appeared on the cover of several magazines, such as Sports Illustrated and Time.
c. By the time she was 8 years old, she had won a state championship.
d. She moves to the bars, salutes the judges, and mounts.

26. Which sentence contains an error in verb tense?

a. Gabby very quickly became close to the Parton family and even considers herself to be a "big sister" to the Parton's four daughters.
b. Chow is a trainer known all over the world for turning American gymnasts into Olympic champions and gold medalists.
c. Gabby Douglas arrived at the 2012 Olympic Games in London, England, as an underdog, but she left the competition as not only a world champion, but also America's sweetheart.
d. During the London Olympics, Gabby stood out as a star, not only for her gymnastic skills, but also for her fun personality and support of the other members of the US team.

27. Which revision corrects the redundancy in the following sentence?

"Gabby, born on December 31, 1995, in Virginia Beach, Virginia, began her formal gymnastics training at the age of 6 years old."

a. Gabby, who was born on December 31, 1995, in Virginia Beach, Virginia, started training gymnastics when she was 6 years old.
b. Gabby, born in Virginia Beach, Virginia, on December 31, 1995, began her training when she was 6 years old.
c. Gabby, born December 31, 1995, in Virginia Beach, Virginia, had begun her training in gymnastics when she was 6 years old.
d. Gabby, born on December 31, 1995, in Virginia Beach, Virginia, began her formal gymnastics training at the age of six.

28. What is the best synonym for "mesmerized" in the sentence below?

"The 4'11", 16-year-old young lady mesmerized the world with her power, flexibility, and form."

a. Ignored
b. Captivated
c. Confused
d. Frightened

Answers and Explanations for Language Test #1

1. A: This passage gives facts about pandas. The introduction should clearly introduce the central idea. Choice A is correct because it lets the reader know that the passage is about pandas and explains why this is a good topic. Choices B and C are incorrect because they do not properly introduce the main idea of the passage. They could each introduce a paragraph in the body of the essay. However, both sentences are too specific to be the first sentence in the passage. Choice D contains information that distracts the reader from the central idea. This sentence does not make it clear what the central idea is, so choice D is incorrect.

2. its eyes: In sentence 4, the passage states that baby pandas cannot open their eyes for the first two months of life. It also says that, because of this, baby pandas rely on their mothers for everything. Sentence 6 says that, even though something about the baby panda has changed, it still relies on its mother for food. This means that the correct choice is *its eyes*. The sentence lets the reader know that, even though the panda can open its eyes, it is still dependent on its mother for some of its needs. The passage does not suggest that the panda cannot open its mouth or move its arms before this point. It does not make sense to say that the baby panda's friends are open.

3. D: Sentence 7 tells how often baby pandas receive food from their mothers. Sentence 8 states that baby pandas chew on bamboo for fun. The sentence added between these sentences should support sentence 7 and make sense in this location. Choice D explains that baby pandas receive food from their mothers often because they need nutrients from the food so that they can grow. This sentence makes sense between sentences 7 and 8 because it is about panda's diets. It supports the information in sentence 7 and flows logically to the information in sentence 8, so choice D is correct. Choices A and B are about the abilities that baby pandas gain between the first 18 months of their lives. However, sentences 7 and 8 are both related to baby pandas' diets. A sentence about their ability to look around or walk would not make much sense between these sentences This means choices A and B are incorrect. Choice C is about mother pandas. This also does not make sense between sentences 7 and 8 because they are about baby pandas' diets. This makes choice C incorrect.

4. B: Paragraph 3 is about pandas during the first 12 to 18 months of their lives. Most of the information in the paragraph pertains to pandas' diets at this stage in their lives. The first sentence in the paragraph should introduce this topic. Choice B is correct because sentence 11 talks about pandas' first 12 to 18 months and says that they start eating bamboo. This is a logical introductory sentence to this paragraph. Sentence 10 adds information to what is stated in sentence 11, so sentence 11 should come first. This means choice A is incorrect. The information about pandas staying near their mothers makes more sense after the information about bamboo. This means that choices C and D are incorrect.

5. D: Since paragraph 1 is the introduction, it should prepare the reader for the rest of the passage. Currently, the introduction tells the reader that the narrator loves bubblegum and has a whole bag of it to chew. The rest of the passage tells about what happens when the narrator gets some of this gum stuck in her hair. The last sentence of the introduction should prepare the reader for this aspect of the story. Choice D suggests that something will happen with the bubblegum. Choice D is correct because adding it to the end of the introduction would help that paragraph prepare the reader for the rest of the story. The flavors of the bubblegum do not prepare the reader for the rest of the story, so choice A is incorrect. How often the narrator is allowed to chew bubblegum also does not prepare the reader for the story, so choice B is incorrect. The times that the narrator will chew bubblegum are also not helpful for the reader to know, so choice C is incorrect.

6. B: A sentence added after sentence 8 will need to make sense between sentences 8 and 9. It will also need to support the meaning of sentence 8. In sentence 8, the narrator is enjoying her afternoon. In sentence 9, she realized that she does not know where her bubblegum is. The narrator likely feels very different in sentence 9 than she did in sentence 8. Choice B shows this change. Choice B shows that something happened and interrupted the narrator's perfect afternoon. It also prepares the reader for the problem in sentence 9, so choice B is correct. The flavor of the bubblegum is not related to the ideas in sentence 8 or sentence 9, so choice A is incorrect. Choices C and D are both incorrect because, though the sandwich or blanket may have helped the narrator enjoy the afternoon, they do not belong between sentences 8 and 9.

7. A: In sentence 22, the narrator and her mother go to the kitchen to get ice. However, the sentence currently repeats the fact that they went to the kitchen. It is best that the sentence starts by telling the reader that they went to the kitchen. This helps the reader understand the order of events and actions of the characters in the story. Answer choices B, C, and D are all redundant and have grammatical errors.

8. C: In sentence 24, the narrator's mother explains that the ice will make the gum harden. She adds that this will make the gum less sticky and easier to remove. In sentences 27 and 28, the narrator's mother is able to remove some of the gum and tells the narrator that the ice helped a little. This shows that the narrator's mother was right about the effects of the ice on the gum. The gum did harden, so choice C is correct. Choice B is the opposite of what happened, so it is incorrect. Choice A says that the gum came out. Sentence 27 shows that not all of the gum came out after the gum hardened, so choice A is incorrect. While the narrator's mother's hands may have become cold, this detail does not show why some of the gum came out. Choice D does not add clarity, so it is incorrect.

9. C: Sentence 2 is a compound sentence. Compound sentences are made of two independent clauses. Independent clauses must be joined using a semicolon or a comma and a coordinating conjunction. Sentence 2 already contains the coordinating conjunction *but*. However, it does not contain a comma. This means that choice C is correct, since a comma should be added between *them* and *but*. *Worries* is only used with singular nouns. *People* is a plural noun, so *worry* is the correct verb to use with it. This means choice A is incorrect. *Bit* is a past tense verb, so it cannot be used with *will*. This makes choice B incorrect. To feed on something means to get food from it. To feed with something means to eat with it. Changing *on* to *with* in sentence 2 would not make sense, since the sentence is saying that bats do not get food from people. This means choice D is incorrect.

10. C: Adjectives that end in *-er* are comparative adjectives. This means that they are used to compare two things. In sentence 7, the author is simply describing the juice from the flowers. The author is not comparing this juice to anything else, so *sweeter* is not the best word to use here. *Sweeter* should be changed to *sweet*, so choice C is correct. Choice A suggests changing the plural noun *bats* to the singular noun *bat*. This sentence is talking about more than one bat, so choice A is incorrect. *Drinks* is a verb that is used in present tense, and *drank* is a verb that is used in past tense. Sentence 7 is in present tense, so choice B is incorrect. The word *flowers* is not used to show that the flower owns or possesses something, so an apostrophe is not needed. This makes choice D incorrect.

11. B: Sentence 8 includes a misspelled word. *Mammuls* should be changed to *mammals*, so choice B is correct. The verb *are* is used in the present tense, and the verb *were* is used in the past tense.

Sentence 8 is in present tense, so *are* is the correct verb to use in this sentence. This makes choice A incorrect. The verb *flies* is singular, so it should be used with singular nouns. Sentence 8 is talking about all bats, so a plural verb should be used. *Fly* can be used as a plural verb, so choice C is incorrect. Since there was a misspelled word in sentence 8, choice D is incorrect.

12. B: *Always* means that something happens all of the time. It can also mean that any time it is possible for something to happen, that thing will happen. *Rarely* means that something does not happen very often. Sentence 15 currently says that bats always bite people. This means that any time a bat can bite someone, it will. However, sentence 2 says that bats do not feed on, or get food from, people. Sentence 16 says if bats bite people, they do not take much blood. This shows that there are times that bats do not bite people. *Rarely* should be used instead of *always* to make sentence 15 true, so choice B is correct. There is no reason to add a comma to sentence 15, so choice A is incorrect. *Bites* is a singular verb, so it cannot be used with the plural noun *bats.* This means choice C is incorrect. The word *people* is used correctly in sentence 15, so choice D is incorrect.

13. A: Weather and *whether* are homophones, so they sound the same but have different meanings. The word *weather* refers to climate or the conditions outdoors. The word *whether* is used to show multiple possibilities. Sentence 2 says that musical sounds can come from either a violin or an electric guitar. These are two possibilities, so the correct word to use is *whether.* This means choice A is correct. Sentence 2 uses the verb *is. Is* is a singular verb, so it must be used with a singular noun. *Instrument* is a singular noun, and *instruments* is a plural noun. *Instruments* cannot be used with the verb *is*, so choice B is incorrect. Choice C says that the word *electric* should be capitalized. In this sentence, *electric* is not used as a proper noun, so it does not need to be capitalized. This makes choice C incorrect. *Strings* is a plural noun, but *string's* is a possessive noun. The strings mentioned in sentence 2 do not own or "possess" anything, so choice D is incorrect.

14. B: Sentence 3 explains why the sounds made by instruments can be heard. The sentence only describes one reason for this, so sentence 3 should use a singular noun. *Reasons* is a plural noun, and *reason* is a singular noun, so choice B is correct. The word *sound* is spelled using the vowel team *ou*, so choice A is incorrect. The pronoun *they* is a subjective pronoun, so it is used as the subject of a sentence. *Them* is an objective pronoun, so it is used as the object of a sentence. The pronoun is used in place of the noun *instruments*, which are doing the action in the sentence. This means that a subjective pronoun is needed, so *they* is the correct pronoun. This means choice B is incorrect. The preposition *in* is used to show that something is inside of, throughout, or within something else. The preposition *by* is used to show that something is next to or beside something else. In sentence 3, the vibrations are found throughout the air, so choice D is incorrect.

15. C: Sentence 6 is a simple sentence, so it only has one independent clause. The word *and* appears after the comma, and it is used to connect two items in a list. Since the sentence is a simple sentence, and the conjunction is used to create a list of only two items, no comma is needed after *air*. This makes choice C correct. *These* is used with, or in place of, plural nouns. *This* is used with, or in place of, singular nouns. In sentence 6, *these* is used with the plural noun *sound waves*, so choice A is incorrect. The word *will* is used with verbs to show that they are in future tense. Sentence 6 is in present tense, so it should only include present tense verbs. The word *will* should not be added to sentence 6, so choice B is incorrect. In sentence 6, the ears belong to a person, so the apostrophe and *s* are needed to show that the person possesses the ears. This means choice D is incorrect.

16. D: *Musicul* is a misspelling of the word *musical*, so choice D is correct. The verb *playing*, by itself, is a present tense verb. *Played* is a past tense verb. Sentence 8 is written in present tense, so *playing* is the correct verb to use in sentence 8. This makes choice A incorrect. Sentence 8 contains two independent clauses. Independent clauses must be joined using a semicolon or a comma and a coordinating conjunction. The comma after *waves* is used correctly in this sentence, so choice B is incorrect. The pronoun *us* is an objective pronoun, and the word *we* is used as a subjective pronoun. In this sentence, the pronoun *us* receives the action from the waves. This means that the pronoun is the object of the sentence, so an objective pronoun is needed. This means choice C is incorrect.

17. D: Sentence 9 currently mentions avoiding buying new paper twice. This is repetitive, so one of the mentions should be removed. Removing the portion in choice A would leave the following sentence: "Or a canvas, you can paint directly on old paper, so you don't have to buy paper." The beginning of this sentence is not clear or correct, since it begins with "or a canvas." Removing the portion in choice D would leave the following sentence: "Instead of buying new paper or a canvas, you can paint directly on old paper." This sentence makes sense, is written correctly, and does not contain repeated information. This makes choice D correct. Choices B and C both contain information that is only stated once, so neither choice would correct the error.

18. B: Sentence 11 explains what a mosaic is, but it also says they are mostly made of glass or stone. Sentence 12 says that colorful paper can be used to make the pieces of a mosaic. A sentence placed between sentences 11 and 12 should connect these two ideas. Choice B says that a paper mosaic involves using pieces of paper rather than pieces of glass or stone. Choice B connects the ideas in sentences 11 and 12, is related to the rest of the paragraph, and is a relevant supporting detail. This means choice B is correct. The passage is about recycling paper, so choice A is irrelevant and incorrect. Choices C and D contain details that are related to the information in sentence 11. However, neither sentence supports the paragraph, so choices C and D are incorrect.

19. C: Sentence 22 is the introductory sentence of paragraph 4. Later in this paragraph, sentence 23 says that origami involves folding paper into objects, such as figurines. Sentences 24 and 25 show that paper can also be used to make origami decorations and supplies. This shows that this paragraph is about folding paper to make objects. The introductory sentence should tell the reader that this paragraph is about folding paper to create small objects, so choice C is correct. The paragraph is about folding paper into many different objects, not just paper airplanes. This means that choice A is incorrect. The point of folding paper into small objects is to avoid throwing it away, so choice B is incorrect. The specific instructions for folding paper to make objects are not discussed in this paragraph, so choice D is incorrect.

20. A: Paragraph 4 is about folding paper to create small objects. Sentence 26 mentions glue, but this information supports the information given earlier in the paragraph. Sentence 27 gives more information about using glue. This is off topic and is not a good concluding sentence for this paragraph. Choice A is correct because it is about making paper objects, which is the main subject of the paragraph, and it wraps up the paragraph effectively. Choice B repeats the information given in sentence 26, so it is incorrect. Choice C is about glue, so it is also off topic and, therefore, incorrect. Choice D is about making things from paper, but it introduces a new idea that does not support the information in the paragraph. It is not a good conclusion for this paragraph, so choice D is incorrect.

21. C: The word *between* is spelled using the vowel team *ee*, not the vowel team *ea*. It is misspelled in sentence 3, so choice C is correct. The verb *can* is used to show that something is able to complete an action. Male polar bears are able to weigh 800 to 1500 pounds, so the word *can* is used correctly. This means choice A is incorrect. Changing *from* to *with* would change the meaning of the sentence, and it would not make sense. This makes choice B incorrect. There is no need to add a comma after *eight*, so choice D is incorrect.

22. B: *Spent* is a verb that is used in past tense, and *spend* is a verb that is used in present tense. Sentence 4 is in present tense, so choice B is correct. This sentence is about more than one bear, so the plural noun *bears* is used correctly in sentence 4. This means choice A is incorrect. The pronoun *their* is used to show possession, but the pronoun *there* is used to describe a location. Since this sentence is talking about the time that belongs to the polar bears, *their* is used correctly in this sentence, meaning choice C is incorrect. Since *spent* should be changed to *spend*, choice D is incorrect.

23. and: The first clause in the sentence tells what purpose polar bears' fur has. The second clause tells what purpose their claws and teeth have. The second clause adds to the information from the first clause, so *and* is the correct choice. Polar bears have thick fur, strong claws, and strong teeth, so *or* and *nor* would be incorrect in this sentence. The word *so* shows that something is the reason for something else. Polar bears' fur does not cause them to have strong claws and teeth, so *so* is also an incorrect choice.

24. A: Polar bears have both big feet and big claws. They do not just have one or the other. This means that *or* should be changed to *and* in sentence 14. This makes choice A correct. The verb *allow*, by itself, is used in present tense. The word *allowed* is used in past tense. Sentence 14 is in present tense, so choice B is incorrect. The word *without* is a compound word, so it is spelled correctly. This means choice C is incorrect. The word *slipping* is spelled using a double consonant, so choice D is incorrect.

25. B: A compound sentence contains two independent clauses separated by a comma and a conjunction or a semicolon. The only answer choice that correctly has this is option B.

26. A: Answer choice A switches from past tense to present tense. "Gabby very quickly became close" is past tense, but "considers" is present tense. An alternate version that would revise this error could be "Gabby very quickly became close to the Parton family and even considered herself to be a "big sister" to the Parton's four daughters."

27. D: The phrase "at the age of 6 years old" is redundant because "6 years old" already conveys the age. The most concise and grammatically correct revision is answer choice D.

28. B: The word "mesmerized" means to hold someone's attention completely, much like the word "captivated" does.

Reading Practice Test #2

Questions 1–11 pertain to the following passage:

That Was Then, and This Is Now

(1) Becca slumped on Grandma's flowered sofa. She loved Grandma, but her house was so dull. Becca was bored.

(2) "Grandma, there's nothing to do!" Becca whined.

(3) "You could watch TV," Grandma suggested.

(4) "There's nothing to watch on your channels. Why don't you have cable?" Becca asked.

(5) "I don't need cable," Grandma said. "When I was little, there were only three television stations available. In fact, we didn't even have a TV until I was 12 years old. And even then, it was black-and-white."

(6) "That sounds awful," Becca said.

(7) "Actually, we thought it was wonderful," Grandma said. "But that was then, and this is now."

(8) "Well, what about getting a game system or a computer. That would give me something to do when I'm here," Becca said.

(9) "We didn't have computers or game systems when I was young," Grandma said. "But we always managed to keep ourselves quite busy."

(10) "You must have been so bored all the time," Becca said. "What did you do to keep busy?"

(11) "Oh, we played outside. We rode our bikes, and sometimes we stuck playing cards in the spokes of the wheels to make them sound like motorcycles. We went fishing and built forts out of blankets or scrap wood or whatever else we could find. Yes, we kept busy." Grandma smiled, remembering.

(12) "I guess that doesn't sound so bad," Becca said. "But what if it was raining, like today? Then you couldn't do any of those things."

(13) "On rainy days, we played inside games," Grandma said. "We played checkers and solitaire and other games. We read books for hours. We made paper dolls and designed whole wardrobes for them. But I guess that was then, and this is now."

(14) "Wow," said Becca. "That sounds kind of fun. What else was different way back then?"

(15) Grandma laughed. "It wasn't all that long ago, Becca. But many things were different."

(16) Grandma told Becca about having fresh milk delivered to her doorstep in glass bottles instead of buying it in plastic jugs at the supermarket. She talked about wearing dresses to school every day instead of jeans and T-shirts. She talked about using pay phones instead of cell phones. She talked about listening to soap operas on the radio instead of watching them on TV. She talked about playing records and dancing the twist.

(17) "But that was then," Grandma said, "and this is now."

(18) Becca was amazed. "You're right, Grandma. Practically everything is different now. It seems like the whole world has changed since you were my age."

(19) Grandma shook her head. "Not everything has changed, Becca. Some things will never change."

(20) "Like what?" Becca asked.

(21) "Well," Grandma answered, "back then grandmas loved their granddaughters, just like I love you now."

(22) Becca leaned over and hugged Grandma tightly. "I love you, too," she said. "Now, how about a game of checkers?"

(23) Grandma smiled. "Sounds good. Maybe things haven't changed so much after all!"

(24) They played checkers, and Grandma beat Becca all three games. Then they used pillows and blankets and all six dining room chairs to build a massive fort in the living room. They sat in the dim fort and had a picnic lunch of sandwiches and chocolate chip cookies. After lunch, Grandma showed Becca how to make paper dolls and design clothes for them. The afternoon flew past.

(25) When Becca's mom came to pick her up, Becca did not want to go home.

(26) "But I thought you were bored," Grandma said.

(27) Becca grinned. "Oh, Grandma," she said, "I was bored. But that was then, and this is now!"

1. Where does this story take place?

a. At Becca's house
b. At Grandma's house
c. At a vacation house
d. At Becca's mom's house

2. Which of the following best represents the main theme of this story?

a. There are many different ways to have fun.
b. Becca is bored all the time.
c. Grandma is old and dull.
d. Activities from the past are not exciting.

3. What word does the author use in paragraph 1 to describe Becca's feelings about Grandma's house?

a. Exciting
b. Tolerable
c. Dull
d. Boring

4. Part A: What is the difference between Becca's attitude at the beginning of the story and her attitude at the end?

a. There is no difference in her attitude
b. She is bored at the beginning of the story and not bored at the end
c. She is angry with Grandma at the beginning of the story and happy with her at the end
d. She is excited at the beginning of the story and bored at the end

Part B: What makes her change her attitude?

a. Nothing, she has no attitude change.
b. Grandma makes her lunch
c. Grandma tells her about all the fun things she did as a kid.
d. Grandma takes her home

5. Which of the following does the story say Grandma did to keep busy when she was young? Select all that apply.

a. Use a computer
b. Play outside
c. Went fishing
d. Watch color TV
e. Build a fort

6. What is the author's main purpose in writing this story?

a. To entertain
b. To inform
c. To persuade
d. To influence

7. Which of the following is a statement of fact?

a. Black-and-white TV is boring
b. Grandma is a dull person
c. Milk used to be delivered in glass bottles
d. Playing outside is exciting

8. Where do Grandma and Becca eat their lunch in this story?

a. Outside on the lawn
b. In a blanket fort
c. At the dining table
d. At a restaurant

9. Part A: Which of the following does Becca ask Grandma to get in this story?

a. A dog
b. A TV
c. A car
d. A computer

Part B: What was Grandma's reason for not getting one?

a. They were too expensive
b. They were too much upkeep
c. She didn't have one when she was younger
d. She just didn't want one

10. Which character in this story has the most positive attitude?

a. Becca
b. Grandma
c. Becca's mom
d. No one in the story has a positive attitude

11. Which paragraph is the first to show a definite change in Becca's attitude?

a. Paragraph 10
b. Paragraph 22
c. Paragraph 24
d. Paragraph 26

Questions 12–17 pertain to the passage "The Tradition of Dance":

The Tradition of Dance

(1) It is estimated that there are over 300 Native American tribes, and each of them uses dancing to communicate culture. Native American dances date back hundreds of years and come in many different forms. Different tribes use dance for different purposes and to convey different messages.

(2) Although each dance is different, they all have meanings that are rooted in ancient tradition. The Iroquois performed a corn husk dance to bring good crops and many healthy babies to the tribe. The Choctaw women danced with medicine men to bring their tribe victory in sporting events. The Plains Indians offered thanks to the gods through their Sun Dance, and the Cherokee celebrated both peace and war with the Eagle Dance. During the Snake Ceremonial, Hopi dancers even held live snakes in their mouths before releasing them into the desert to bring rain and a good harvest.

(3) Each of the many different dances also requires a unique costume. These costumes vary widely, but—just like the dances—each has a special meaning. Most dance costumes include a headdress and special ceremonial clothing. Some also include a wand, jewelry, and even body paint. In addition, feathers are often used in costumes to symbolize human traits. One of the most common feathers used is the eagle feather, which represents strength in many tribes.

(4) Though many of the Native American dances are now performed only in ceremonies and at powwows, they remain an important element of Native American culture. These dances are a language, rich in history and meaning. They are passed from generation to generation and will always be a vital part of Native American tradition.

12. How many tribes does the story refer to by name?

a. 3
b. 5
c. 7
d. 8

13. What is the main purpose of dance in the Native American culture?

a. To provide exercise
b. To communicate a message
c. To entertain children
d. To prepare for battle

14. According to paragraph 2, what is the similarity between the Iroquois corn husk dance and the Hopi Snake Ceremonial?

a. They were both intended to bring good crops
b. They both involved women and medicine men
c. They both involved the use of snakes
d. They both involved the use of corn husks

15. Which of the following statements are facts? Select all that apply.

a. Many Native American costumes include a wand and jewelry
b. The dances are passed from generation to generation
c. Ceremonial headdresses make dancers look important
d. These dances date back hundreds of years
e. Eagle feathers are the best feathers

16. What does the eagle feather represent in many Native American tribes?

a. Power
b. Wealth
c. Strength
d. Authority

17. What was the author's main purpose in writing this article?

a. To inform
b. To entertain
c. To influence
d. To persuade

Questions 18–24 pertain to the passage: "The Story of My People"

<u>The Story of My People</u>

(1) As we pulled into the community college parking lot, I felt my excitement rising. Powwows were one of my favorite things. I loved the talking, the laughing, the music, and—most of all—the dancing. I loved seeing and hearing and feeling my Cherokee heritage.

(2) Inside the large gymnasium, the powwow was just getting started. My father and grandfather went to join the men who had gathered in the far corner. Around the edges of the gym, women sat behind long tables draped with vibrant cloths. On the tables were items for sale. I wandered around and looked at the leather vests, beaded belts, and beautiful jewelry.

(3) As I came to the end of the tables, I heard behind me the low, pulsing beat of a single drum. It made a hollow, echoing sound. Soon other drums joined the rhythm, filling the air with their deep sound. High-pitched rattles joined in, and a group of men drifted to the center of the floor. The dancing had begun.

(4) I found a seat on some bleachers and watched with wonder. Synchronized steps beat out a perfect rhythm while voices chanted high and low in beautiful unison. Feathers and beads and shiny black braids flashed past as the intensity increased. It was magical to me.

(5) Some dances were for the children; some were for the men or women; some were for everyone. Sometimes tribes danced separately, and sometimes they all danced together. Some dances offered thanks, and others asked for blessings; some were celebrations, and others were prayers. But although each dance was different, they all told a story. It was an ancient story: the story of my people.

18. What tribe represents the heritage of the narrator of this story?

a. Hopi
b. Cherokee
c. Iroquois
d. Choctaw

19. In what point of view is this story written?

a. First person
b. Second person
c. Third person
d. None of the above

20. What is the main theme of this story?

a. Native American dancing tells a story
b. Powwows are exciting
c. Community colleges are great places to hold powwows
d. Native American children learn to dance at a young age

21. Which of the following is a statement of opinion?

a. Some dances are designed to bring a blessing
b. Each dance is different, but each has a meaning
c. Many dances involve synchronized steps, music, and chanting
d. Native American dancing is emotionally powerful

22. What does the narrator do before the dancing begins?

a. Buys snacks at the snack bar
b. Looks at the tables of items for sale
c. Takes a walk around the campus
d. Practices different dancing steps

23. What is the meaning of the word "pulsing" as it appears in paragraph 3?

a. a steady or rhythmic beat
b. a sudden loud noise
c. the seeds of a plant
d. a beating heart

24. The narrator says that the dancing tells a story. What was that story?

a. the story of the eagle
b. the story of his people
c. the story of great harvest
d. the story of happiness

Questions 25–27 pertain to both passages "The Tradition of Dance" and "The Story of My People"

25. What main theme is central to both stories?

a. The value of powwows in Native American culture
b. The focus on family in Native American culture
c. The importance of dancing in Native American culture
d. The power of medicine men in Native American culture

26. What is Native American dancing compared to in both stories?

a. Language
b. Music
c. Cooking
d. Art

27. Which tribe was mentioned in both stories?

a. Choctaw
b. Hopi
c. Cherokee
d. Iroquois

Questions 28–40 pertain to the following passage:

In Abuela's World

(1) In June, just after school ended, Marianna and her family went to see her abuela—her grandmother—in Tampico, Mexico. By the time they reached Abuela's small house by the sea, Marianna was exhausted. Abuela put a thick mat on the floor for a bed, and Marianna stretched out and went to sleep.

(2) When Marianna awoke the next morning, the sun was already high in the sky. The air was warm and sticky. Marianna rubbed her eyes and wandered into Abuela's kitchen. Delicious smells bubbled up from a pot on the stove.

(3) "Buenos dias, sleepyhead," Abuela said with a grin. "You must have been tired. You slept half the day away."

(4) Marianna stretched and yawned as her mother came into the kitchen. "What are we doing today, Mami?" Marianna asked.

(5) "Papi and Jorge and I are going down to the beach soon," Mami answered. "You can come with us or stay here with Abuela."

(6) Marianna chose the beach. As she lay in the sun, she listened to the waves. Sea birds called overhead, and the gentle sea breeze kissed her face. It was a perfect afternoon.

(7) The next day, Abuela joined them as they drove south to visit some Aztec ruins. Although the Aztec people once ruled the area of Mexico where Abuela lived, they were conquered by the Spaniards long ago. Crumbling ruins were all that remained of their ancient civilization. Marianna had read about the Aztecs in school. It was amazing to think these stones were once part of the great Aztec empire.

(8) On her third full day in Mexico, Marianna saw her cousins. The three boys shyly greeted Marianna. Then they turned to her younger brother, Jorge.

(9) "Want to play some futbol, Jorge?" they asked.

(10) Jorge nodded. He knew futbol meant soccer in Spanish, and he loved soccer. Marianna went out to watch the boys play. She liked soccer, too, but it was too hot to play in the blazing sun.

(11) Marianna sat on the shady porch and watched the boys kick the ball in the dusty street. The boys played hard, and Marianna found herself cheering for Jorge's team. As the sun went down, they called it a tie and finally headed inside.

(12) The visit to Abuela's world flew by. On the day before she had to leave, Marianna found Abuela in the kitchen.

(13) "I don't want to go home," Marianna said. "I love you, and I love Mexico."

(14) Abuela smiled. "I love you, too. But you would eventually miss your life in America. And you can always come to visit."

(15) "I guess so," said Marianna. "But I'll miss Mexico."

(16) "I know," said Abuela, taking Marianna's hand. "So to help you take Mexico with you, we are having a grand fiesta tonight. Come shopping with me."

(17) They went to the open market where vendors spread their goods on blankets on the ground. Abuela selected items for the party, greeting many of the vendors by name. Then she bought Marianna some chicle, Mexican gum made from sapodilla pulp.

(18) That night, dozens of neighbors, friends, and family members came to the party. They talked and laughed and danced to the mariachi music. Abuela made incredible food for everyone. There was chicken with sweet and spicy mole, enchiladas with rich sauce, rice, fruit, and plenty of tortillas. It was a true feast.

(19) The party went late into the night. Marianna felt she had barely slept when Papi shook her awake and told her it was time to go. As they drove away, Marianna waved to Abuela. Although she was going home, Marianna knew her heart would always hold a special place for Abuela's world.

28. What is the Spanish word for grandmother?

a. Amiga
b. Abuela
c. Alla
d. Alegra

29. Where is the main setting for this story?

a. In the southwest
b. In Tampico, Mexico
c. At the ruins
d. In the open market

30. Which choice best finishes the following chart of events on Marianna's vacation?

Marianna goes to the beach.	⇨	Marianna visits the ruins.	⇨	Marianna sees her cousins.	⇨	Marianna visits the open market.	⇨	

a. Marianna visits a mountain.
b. Marianna takes a road trip through Mexico.
c. Marianna attends a big party at her grandmother's house.
d. Marianna watches the boys play soccer.

31. Part A: Which paragraphs discuss Marianna's visit with her cousins?

a. Paragraph 5 through paragraph 9
b. Paragraph 6 through paragraph 10
c. Paragraph 7 through paragraph 10
d. Paragraph 8 through paragraph 11

Part B: Based on your answer from Part A which event also happened in these paragraphs?

a. Marianna visited the beach
b. Jorge played soccer with his cousins
c. Marianna and her family visited the Aztec ruins
d. Marianna and Abuela went to the market

32. Which word is the best English translation for the Spanish word "futbol"?

a. Football
b. Soccer
c. Baseball
d. Kickball

33. Why did the author tell this story from Marianna's point of view?

a. To help the reader can understand Marianna's thoughts and feelings.
b. There was no other main character in the story.
c. All good stories are written in third-person point of view.
d. This story is not written from Marianna's point of view.

34. Why does the story say Marianna doesn't want to leave Mexico?

a. She hates the long trip.
b. She doesn't have to go to school in Mexico.
c. She loves her grandmother, and she loves Mexico.
d. She likes the weather at the beach.

35. In paragraph 6, which literary device is used to describe the wind?

a. Simile
b. Personification
c. Metaphor
d. No literary device is used

36. Which word best describes the relationship between Marianna and her grandmother?

a. Tense
b. Distant
c. Polite
d. Loving

37. Which of the following is a statement of opinion?

a. Grandmother made chicken with mole for the party
b. Mariachi music was played at the party
c. The food at the party was incredible
d. Neighbors, friends, and family members attended the party

38. Where did Marianna go with her grandmother on the day of the party?

a. To the open market
b. To the beach
c. To the ruins
d. To the supermarket

39. According to the story, what is the main ingredient of chicle?

a. Chicken
b. Chocolate
c. Sugar and spices
d. Sapodilla pulp

40. When did the boys stop playing soccer?

a. When it was time to eat
b. When it was time for bed
c. When one team scored five goals
d. When the sun went down

Answers and Explanations for Reading Test #2

1. B: is the best choice because this story is set at Grandma's house. A, C, and D are not the best choices because they do not accurately represent the setting for the story.

2. A: is the best choice because the main theme of this story is that there are many different ways to have fun. B, C, and D are not the best choices because they are not main themes of the story.

3. C: is the best choice because paragraph 1 indicates that Becca thinks Grandma is "dull". A, B, and D are not the best choices because "dull" is the only word specifically used by the author to describe Becca's feelings about Grandma's house.

4. Part A: B: is the best choice because it most accurately represents the change in Becca's attitude between the beginning and end of the story. A, C, and D are not the best choices because they do not accurately describe the changes in Becca's attitude between the beginning and end of the story.

Part B: C: The point where Becca's attitude starts to change is when Grandma starts telling her about the fun things she did as a kid. Becca decides to do some of these things and she starts having fun.

5. B, C, E: In paragraph 11, Grandma talks about doing all three of these things as a kid.

6. A: is the best choice because the author's main purpose in writing this story is to entertain the reader. B, C, and D are not the best choices because the purpose of the story is not to inform, persuade, or influence.

7. C: is the best choice because it is the only statement of fact. A, B, and D are not the best choices because they are all statements of opinion.

8. B: is the best choice because the story says Becca and Grandma ate lunch in a blanket fort. A, C, and D are not the best choices because they do not accurately describe where Becca and Grandma ate lunch.

9. Part A: D: is the best choice because in paragraph 8 Becca asked Grandma to get a computer. A, B, and C are not the best choices because Becca did not ask Grandma to get a dog, TV, or car.

Part B: C: When Becca asks Grandma for a computer her response is, "We didn't have computers or game systems when I was young,"

10. B: is the best choice because Grandma has the most positive attitude in this story. A and C are not the best choices because Becca and her mom do not clearly demonstrate positive attitudes throughout this story. D is not the best choice because Grandma does have a positive attitude.

11. B: is the best choice because paragraph 22 is the first paragraph to show the change in Becca's attitude. A, C, and D are not the best choices because paragraphs 10, 24, and 26 are not the first paragraphs to show the change in Becca's attitude.

12. B: The five tribes mentioned are the Iroquois, Choctaw, Cherokee, Plains Indians, and Hopi.

13. B: is the best choice because the main purpose of dance in Native American culture is to communicate a message. A, C, and D are not the best choices because they do not accurately reflect the main purpose of dance in Native American culture.

14. A: is the best choice because the Iroquois corn husk dance and the Hopi Snake Ceremonial were both intended to bring good crops. B, C, and D are not the best choices because they do not represent the purpose of these dances.

15. A, B, D: All of these statements can be proven as true and are not debatable.

16. C: is the best choice because in many Native American tribes the eagle feather represents strength. A, B, and D are not the best choices because they do not reflect the meaning of the eagle feather in many Native American tribes.

17. A: is the best choice because the author's main purpose in writing this article is to inform the reader. B, C, and D are not the best choices because the author's primary purpose in writing this article is not to entertain, to influence, or to persuade.

18. B: is the best choice because paragraph 1 indicates the narrator is of Cherokee heritage. A, C, and D are not the best choices because the narrator is not of Hopi, Iroquois, or Choctaw heritage.

19. A: is the best choice because this story is written in first person. B, C, and D are not the best choices because they do not accurately represent the point of view in which this story is written.

20. A: is the best choice because the main theme of this story is that Native American dancing tells a story. B, C, and D are not the best choices because they do not accurately represent the main theme of this story.

21. D: is the best choice because it is the only statement of opinion. A, B, and C are not the best choices because they are all statements of fact.

22. B: is the best choice because the story indicates the narrator was looking at the items for sale on the tables before the dancing began. A, C, and D are not the best choices because they do not accurately reflect what the narrator was doing before the dancing began.

23. A: "Pulsing" refers to the steady beating of the drum.

24. B: The last sentence of the story states, "It was an ancient story: the story of my people."

25. C: is the best choice because the importance of dancing in the Native American culture is a central theme in both stories. A, B, and D are not the best choices because they do not represent themes that are central to both stories.

26. A: is the best choice because both stories compare Native American dancing to language. B, C, and D are not the best choices because Native American dancing is not compared in these stories to music, cooking, or art.

27. C: The Cherokee are mentioned in the first story and they are the main focus of the second story. None of the others are mentioned in the second story.

28. B: is the best choice because the Spanish word for grandmother is "abuela". A, C, and D are not the best choices because none of these words mean grandmother.

29. B: is the best choice because this story is set in Tampico, Mexico. A, C, and D are not the best choices because they do not represent the true setting of this story.

30. C: is the best choice because it most accurately completes the chart of Marianna's vacation. A, B, and D are not the best choices because they do not accurately complete the chart of Marianna's vacation.

31. Part A: D: is the best choice because paragraphs 8 through 11 discuss Marianna's visit with her cousins. A, B, and C are not the best choices because they do not represent the correct range of paragraphs that discuss Marianna's visit with her cousins.

Part B: B: In paragraph 9, after meeting her cousins, they ask Jorge to play "futbol" or soccer. All of the other events occurred outside of paragraphs 8 through 11.

32. B: is the best choice because futbol means soccer. A, C, and D are not the best choices because they are incorrect translations of futbol.

33. A: is the best choice because the author wrote from Marianna's point of view to show her thoughts and feelings to the reader. B, C, and D are not the best choices because they do not represent the author's intentions in writing from Marianna's point of view.

34. C: is the best choice because paragraph 13 shows Marianna does not want to go home because she loves Abuela and loves Mexico. A, B, and D are not the best choices because they do not accurately reflect why Marianna does not want to leave Mexico.

35. B: is the best choice because paragraph 6 uses personification to describe the wind. A and C are not the best choices because simile and metaphor are not used to describe the wind in paragraph 6. D is not the best choice because personification is used, and personification is a literary device.

36. D: is the best choice because the relationship between Marianna and her grandmother is clearly loving. A, B, and C are not the best choices because they do not accurately describe the relationship between Marianna and her grandmother.

37. C: is the best choice because it is the only statement of opinion. A, B, and D are not the best choices because they are all statements of fact.

38. A: is the best choice because Marianna went to the open market with Abuela on the day of the party. B, C, and D are not the best choices because Marianna did not go to the beach, the ruins, or the supermarket with Abuela on the day of the party.

39. D: is the best choice because the main ingredient of chicle is sapodilla pulp. A, B, and C are not the best choices because they do not represent the main ingredient of chicle.

40. D: In paragraph 11 it says, "As the sun went down, they called it a tie and finally headed inside."

Language Practice Test #2

Questions 1–4 pertain to the following passage:

Did You Forget Something?

(1) Have you ever forgotten to pack something for a vacation? (2) Everyone forgets things sometimes, but sometimes the items that are forgotten are necessary to enjoy the trip. (3) Often, it's easy to replace forgotten items while you are on vacation. (4) However, this can become expensive and take time away from the activities you were looking forward to. (5) Luckily, there are actions you can take to help you remember what you need to pack.

(6) One way to help yourself remember what to pack is to make a list. (7) A good way to make sure nothing is missing from your list is to think through your day. (8) Think about all the things you do to get ready for the day. (9) Write down all of the items you need to do those things. (10) Think about all of the things you need to get ready for bed. (11) You need at night any items that you don't need to add to the list in the morning. (12) Next, write down anything else you need in case of emergency. (13) After you write down the items that you need, you can add the items that you want to take for fun.

(14) Another step you can take to avoid leaving things at home is to categorize them. (15) By laying your items out and grouping them in different categories, you can see how many things you have in each category. (16) This may help you see if anything is missing. (17) For example, imagine you use eight items to get ready for bed, but you only have seven in that category. (18) This will show you that you are missing something in that category. (19) Categorizing your items will also make it easier to find things when you are on vacation. (20) You can keep everything organized in categories within your luggage by using tools like luggage organizers or zipper bags. (21) This will also help you avoid thinking you left something at home, when you really did bring it with you.

(22) A third way to avoid forgetting things at home is to simply double check your luggage before you leave. (23) However, if you take your items out in order to do this, it is very important to make sure that you put everything back in your bag. (24) You can also just double check that you have the things you absolutely need to take on your trip. (25) If you can, put these things where you can easily find them in your luggage. (26) Before you head out, simply open your luggage, make sure you see those items, and close your luggage again. (27) This will help you avoid taking everything out to find them and will help you avoid leaving the most needed items at home.

(28) Paying extra attention as you pack is a good idea. (29) It can lead to a more relaxing vacation. (30) On my trip to Florida last year, I forgot three different things. (31) Next time you are going on vacation, consider taking these steps to make sure you don't forget anything. (32) Doing so can make your vacation go more smoothly so you can enjoy it. (33) Safe travels!

1. Sentence 11 is unclear. Which of the following sentences shows the best version of sentence 11?

a. You need any items at night that you don't need in the morning need to add to the list.
b. To the list you need to add any items that you don't need in the morning you need at night.
c. Add any items that you need at night but don't need in the morning to the list.
d. Any items that you don't need to add to the list in the morning you need at night.

2. Paragraph 2 is missing a concluding sentence. Which of the following sentences would be best to add after sentence 13?

a. You can use these items as you travel to your destination as well as during your stay.
b. Making a list like this can help you think through the things you need to pack so you don't miss anything.
c. Make sure you don't forget to bring anything with you on your trip.
d. Instead of writing your list, you can also type it, which may keep you from losing it.

3. Sentences 28 and 29 should be combined. Which of the following sentences shows the best way to combine these sentences?

a. Paying extra attention as you pack is a good idea, and it can lead to a more relaxing vacation.
b. Paying extra attention as you pack is a relaxing vacation and it can lead to a good idea.
c. Paying extra attention as you pack is a good idea it can lead to a more relaxing vacation.
d. A more relaxing vacation can happen when you pay extra attention as you pack, which is a good idea.

4. Which sentence from the passage is unnecessary and should be removed?

a. Sentence 4
b. Sentence 18
c. Sentence 23
d. Sentence 30

Questions 5–7 pertain to the following passage:

Niagara Falls

(1) Last summer, my family went on a trip to Niagara Falls in New York. (2) Niagara Falls is a famous waterfall that flows between the United States and Canada. (3) When I first saw Niagara Falls, I couldn't believe it. (4) It was huge! (5) I had never seen so much water in my life.

(7) To get a better look at the falls, we decided to take a boat ride to the base of the falls, where the waterfall crashes into the river. (8) We got on a boat with a lot of other people. (9) Everybody was given blue, plastic rain ponchos. (10) As we got closer to the bottom of the falls, I knew why. (11) The water sprayed up like it was raining, and the crash was so loud I couldn't even hear myself yell.

(12) We saw another boat, far below us, headed for the base of Niagara Falls. (13) When the boat ride was over, we drove back to the top of the falls and walked along the sidewalk. (14) The falls were so big that it made the boat look like a toy and the people look like tiny insects. (15) We made sure to be very careful as we walked since we were up so high. (16) The view from above the falls was just as amazing as the view from the boat.

(17) Before we left Niagara Falls, we went to a gift shop. (18) I bought some postcards at the gift shop. (19) When we got home, I used the post cards to make a new page for my scrapbook. (20) I also wrote down some of my memories from the trip. (21) Now I will always remember my trip to Niagara Falls.

5. Which sentence is the best choice as the first sentence of paragraph 3?

a. Sentence 12
b. Sentence 13
c. Sentence 14
d. Sentence 15

6. Which of the following sentences should replace sentence 12 as the concluding sentence for paragraph 2?

a. The ponchos would keep our clothes dry, so we each wore one during the entire boat ride.
b. It was not as loud as some of the thunderstorms that have happened in my hometown.
c. The poncho was unnecessary, so I threw mine away before the boat ride was done.
d. The boat ride was almost like riding a water coaster, and I was not ready for it to end.

7. Which of the following is the best way to combine sentences 17 and 18?

a. Before we left Niagara Falls, we went to a gift shop, I bought some postcards at the gift shop.
b. Before we left Niagara Falls, we went to a gift shop I bought some postcards at the gift shop.
c. Before we left Niagara Falls, we went to a gift shop, and I bought some postcards.
d. Before we left Niagara Falls, we went to a gift shop where I bought some postcards at the gift shop.

Questions 8–11 pertain to the following passage:

Starting an Aquarium

(1) Imagine bright green plants swaying back and forth in blue water. (2) Add in a small castle and some colorful fish swimming around it. (3) If this sounds like something you would enjoy having, you might want to start your own aquarium. (4) An aquarium is a tanks filled with water and plants where you can keep fish. (5) Terrarium fish are easy pets to take care of, if you are careful to choose the right fish and the right aquarium equipment.

(6) Aquarium fish can be divided into four groups: tropical freshwater species, tropical marine species, coldwater freshwater species, and coldwater marine species. (7) Tropical freshwater species are the easier fish to keep because their needs change based on their surroundings and the resources they have available. (8) They are able to adapt to living through different environments. (9) Some tropical freshwater fish include the rosy barb, angelfish, and x-ray fish.

8. Which change would correct the mistake in sentence 4?

a. Change *tanks* to *tank.*
b. Change *with* to *from.*
c. Add a comma after *water.*
d. Change *keep* to *kept.*

9. Which change needs to be made to sentence 5?

a. Change *Terrarium* to *Aquarium.*
b. Change *pets* to *petts.*
c. Change *of* to *with.*
d. Add a comma before *and.*

10. Which change would correct the mistake in sentence 7?

a. Change *freshwater* to *fresh water.*
b. Change *easier* to *easiest.*
c. Change *their* to *they.*
d. Change *have* to *has.*

11. Which change would correct the mistake in sentence 8?

a. Change *are* to *were.*
b. Change *living* to *liveing.*
c. Change *through* to *in.*
d. Change *environments* to *environment.*

Questions 12–15 pertain to the following passage:

San Antonio De Valero

(1) In the early 1700s, people from Spain established missions throughout the land we now know as the state of Texas. (2) One of the most faymous of these missions is San Antonio de Valero, better known by its nickname: the Alamo. (3) This was the most successful mission in the area, it served several purposes for the surrounding communities.

(4) For over a century, the Alamo served as an active mission. (5) Church services were held in the cool, shady buildings, which provided welcome relief from the blazing summer sun. (6) Couples were married at the Alamo. (7) Babies were baptized there. (8) The Alamo also served as a trading post, supply depot, and communication center. (9) In later years, however, the Alamo served its most famous and—arguably—most important role. (10) It was used as a fortress during the texas revolution.

12. Which change would correct the mistake in sentence 2?

a. Change *faymous* to *famous.*
b. Change *is* to *are.*
c. Change *San Antonio de Valero* to *san antonio de valero.*
d. Change *its* to *that's.*

13. Choose the conjunction that should be added after the comma in sentence 3.

This was the most successful mission in the area, ______ it served several purposes for the surrounding communities.

but
or
and
yet

14. Which change needs to be made to sentence 5?

a. Change *were* to *was.*
b. Change *in* to *on.*
c. Change *summer* to *Summer.*
d. This sentence does not need to be changed.

15. Which change would correct the mistake in sentence 10?

a. Change *was* to *were.*
b. Change *fortress* to *fortresses.*
c. Change *during* to *durring.*
d. Change *texas revolution* to *Texas Revolution.*

Questions 16–19 pertain to the following passage:

A Night to Be Remembered

(1) At the beginning of the year, my teacher announced that our school was going to have a speech contest. (2) It sounded like fun. (3) So, I decided to enter. (4) I thought and thought about what to say in my speech. (5) Then, I went to the library to do some research.

(6) I decided to write my speech about the life and accomplishments of Dr. Martin Luther King Jr. (7) He is one of my favorite people, and I was proud of the speech I wrote about him. (8) When I finished it, I read the speech to my parents. (9) My dad once gave a speech to the city council. (10) They loved it!

(11) On the night of the speech contest, I was very nervous. (12) My stomach was flip-flopping, even though I knew my speech by heart. (13) When it was my turn, I took a deep breath, stood up, and gave my speech perfectly. (14) Everyone clapped, and I sat down. (15) Then, I had to wait for the judges' decision.

(16) Several minutes after the last speech was given, the head judge stood up and said that it was a close contest, and everyone had done well. (17) Then, he announced that I won first place! (18) I was so surprised that my head was spinning, and my knees were wobbly. (19) Everyone cheered when my name was called, and my parents took me out for ice cream after we left. (20) It was a night I will never forget.

16. Which sentence does not belong in this story?

a. Sentence 4
b. Sentence 7
c. Sentence 9
d. Sentence 15

17. Which of the following is the best way to combine sentences 2 and 3?

a. It sounded like fun, I decided to enter.
b. It sounded like fun I decided to enter.
c. Because it sounded like fun I decided to enter.
d. It sounded like fun, so I decided to enter.

18. Which sentence would be best to add before sentence 11, at the beginning of paragraph 3?

a. I chose to write about Dr. King because of how he contributed to the Civil Rights Movement.
b. I kept practicing my speech so that I could do my best when it was time for the contest.
c. I finished writing my speech three weeks before the competition.
d. I enjoyed the topic I chose so much that I decided I would use it for my next essay, as well.

19. Which of the following would be a good concluding sentence for paragraph 3?

a. Even though I was eager to hear the judges' decision, I enjoyed listening to my classmates give their speeches.
b. I wonder if I would have done as well if I had chosen a different topic for my speech.
c. My parents were sitting in the second row of the audience, and I sat with them after I gave my speech.
d. My speech was about four minutes long, but a lot of my classmates gave 5-minute-long speeches.

Questions 20–23 pertain to the following passage:

Official Languages

(1) Most countries have at least one official language. (2) Usually, a country's official language is spokeen by most of the people who live in that country. (3) Some countries have multiple official languages. (4) For example, Canada has two official languages: english and french. (5) Two countries may have the same official language, but the language may be spoken differently in each country. (6) For example, French is an official language of both Canada and France. (7) However, the way French is spoken in Canada and the way it is spoken in France are not exactly the same. (8) One big difference is the vocabulary used by French speaker's in each country. (9) The language spoken by a group of people may be an important way that those people identify itself.

20. Which change would correct the mistake in sentence 2?

a. Change *country's* to *countries.*
b. Add a comma after *language.*
c. Change *spokeen* to *spoken.*
d. Change *in* to *from.*

21. Which change would correct the mistake in sentence 4?

a. Change *has* to *had.*
b. Change *two* to *too.*
c. Change *languages* to *language.*
d. Change *english and french* to *English and French.*

22. Which change would correct the mistake in sentence 8?

a. Change *is* to *are.*
b. Add a comma after *used.*
c. Change *French* to *french.*
d. Change *speaker's* to *speakers.*

23. Which change would correct the mistake in sentence 9?

a. Change *group* to *groups.*
b. Change *important* to *most important.*
c. Change *identify* to *identifies.*
d. Change *itself* to *themselves.*

Questions 24–28 pertain to the following passage:

Less Litter

(1) Have you ever been riding in the car and looked outside at the scenery? The scenery, whether it is a landscape or the middle of a city, can be beautiful, but it can also be spoiled by litter. When people litter, they can cause harm to the areas around them. It is very important to make sure you dispose of trash properly rather than dropping or tossing it on the ground.

(2) One reason to avoid littering is that litter can harm animals. When litter is thrown into the grass, left on the beach, or dropped on walking trails, animals may find it and try to eat it. Animals cannot always tell what they are eating, and if they eat trash, it can injure them or make them sick.

(3) Litter can also hurt plants. Plants use their roots to absorb nutrients from the soil. When trash is left on the ground, it may get buried in the dirt. This means that plants' roots will be blocked by the trash, and they may absorb chemicals from the buried trash. The trash can also prevent water from soaking into the ground, which also hurts plants. When trash is placed in a trashcan, it is less likely to harm plants and animals.

(4) In addition to causing harm to plants and animals, litter can also harm people and the environment. When litter is thrown out, no matter where it lands, strong winds or animals may carry it to bodies of water. When litter gets in the water, it pollutes it. Some trash may be decorated using dye or ink. Dye and ink can dissolve in the water and become difficult to remove from it. Over time, plastic will break down in water, so it also becomes difficult to take out of the water. When polluted water flows through an area, it affects nearby plants, animals, and soil.

(5) This water is also brought into water treatment centers, where it is filtered, or cleaned, so it can be used in houses and other buildings. However, when water is very polluted, not all of the things polluting the water can be removed from it. This means they can end up in our drinking water. The chemicals and debris that may be left in drinking water can be harmful to humans. Litter is not the only thing that pollutes water, but reducing the amount of litter can help decrease water pollution.

(6) Litter also distracts from the beauty of the scenery around us. Wildflowers that grow by the side of the highway are beautiful. However, when people toss trash from their cars, then cans, wrappers, and other trash surround and cover these flowers. This is also true of sand on the beach or plants in the forest. Litter often takes people's attention away from the natural scenes around them.

(7) Urban areas like cities can also be beautiful, but only when they are kept clean. Litter on sidewalks is unpleasant to see, may smell bad, and can get in the way of people walking through a city. Whether litter is left in nature or in a town or city, it is often upsetting to see. Litter can disrupt people who want to focus on the beauty around them.

(8) Litter can have a negative impact on both our health and the world around us. Even though we cannot always avoid having trash, we can be careful about what we do with it. Next time you are outside and have something to throw away, hold onto

it until you can find a trash can and throw it away properly. Reducing litter is an important way to help keep the areas around us clean, healthy, and beautiful.

24. What is the best synonym for "disrupt" in the sentence below?

"Litter can disrupt people who want to focus on the beauty around them."

a. Improve
b. Disturb
c. Assist
d. Impress

25. What revision makes the following sentences more concise?

"Some trash may be decorated using dye or ink. Dye and ink can dissolve in the water and become difficult to remove from it."

a. Some trash may have dye or ink that dissolves in water and is difficult to remove from the water.
b. Some trash may be decorated using dye or ink, which the dye or ink will dissolve, and it will be difficult to remove from the water.
c. Dye or ink can dissolve and become difficult to remove from water.
d. Trash can be decorated using harmful dye or ink that dissolve in the water.

26. Which of the following is a compound sentence?

a. Litter can have a negative impact on both our health and the world around us.
b. Litter on sidewalks is unpleasant to see, may smell bad, and can get in the way of people walking through a city.
c. The scenery, whether it is a landscape or the middle of a city, can be beautiful, but it can also be spoiled by litter.
d. Litter often takes people's attention away from the natural scenes around them.

27. The passage "Less Litter" is best described as what type of text?

a. Narrative
b. Expository
c. Persuasive
d. Instructional

28. Which option best combines the following sentences?

"This means they can end up in our drinking water. The chemicals and debris that may be left in drinking water can be harmful to humans."

a. This means that the things left, such as chemicals and debris, can end up in our drinking water can be harmful to humans.
b. This means that the chemicals and debris can end up in our drinking water.
c. The chemicals and debris, in our drinking water, are harmful.
d. Humans can be harmed by chemicals and debris that are left because the chemicals and debris don't get removed from the drinking water.

Answers and Explanations for Language Test #2

1. C: Sentence 11 is currently unclear. It should be replaced with a sentence that is clear, makes sense, and contains the same information. Choice C is correct because it makes sense and contains all of the information from the original version of sentence 11. Choices A and B are incorrect because they do not make sense. Choice D makes sense, but it has the wrong meaning and is not written very clearly.

2. B: Choice B closes the paragraph in a way that reminds the reader of the main point of the paragraph and shows how the supporting details are related. This makes choice B correct. Choice A is a supporting detail about the items mentioned in sentence 13. While this sentence is related to sentence 13, it does not conclude the paragraph well, so choice A is incorrect. This paragraph gives the reader a useful method for avoiding leaving things at home. Choice C simply tells the reader not to forget things. This sentence does not belong in this passage because the purpose of the passage is to prevent readers from having this attitude when packing for a trip. This means choice C is incorrect. Choice D is a supporting detail that is relevant to the paragraph. However, it only adds more information and does not conclude the sentence well, so choice D is incorrect.

3. A: Choice A is correct because it combines sentences 28 and 29 in a clear way and uses correct grammar. It also has the same meaning as sentences 28 and 29. Choice B is incorrect because it does not have the same meaning as sentences 28 and 29. It says that paying attention is a vacation, which is not true. Choice C is incorrect because it is a run-on sentence. Choice D is incorrect because it is unclear.

4. D: Sentence 30 is unnecessary because it simply states that the author forgot items on a trip. This detail does not support the ideas or points made in the passage. This makes choice D correct. Choice A is incorrect because sentence 4 is a supporting detail that shows why replacing forgotten items can still interrupt a vacation. Choice B is incorrect because sentence 18 explains why the method described in sentences 15 and 16 is helpful. Choice C is incorrect because sentence 23 gives an important clarification about the method described in sentence 22.

5. B: Most of this passage is told in chronological order, so this order should be maintained throughout the passage. Paragraph 3 is about the narrator seeing people on a boat far below. Since paragraph 2 was about the narrator being on a boat, the events in paragraph 2 must take place in a different location. Sentence 13 shows that the narrator and his or her family left the boat and traveled to the top of Niagara Falls. Sentence 13 is correct because the event described in this sentence must have occurred before the events described in the rest of the paragraph. The events in sentences 12, 14, and 15 occurred at the top of the falls, so they happened after the narrator traveled from the boat. This means that choices A, C, and D are incorrect.

6. D: Paragraph 2 is about the narrator's experience on a boat ride at Niagara Falls. Choice D is correct because it states the narrator's opinion of the boat ride. This is a good concluding idea for this paragraph. Choice A is incorrect because it does not fit well in the paragraph. Additionally, the information in this sentence is implied, or suggested, by sentence 11. Choice B is incorrect because it is not relevant to the passage. This detail does not help the reader understand the events in the passage. It is not a good concluding idea for paragraph 2. Choice C is incorrect because it contains information that is not supported by the passage. Sentence 10 shows that the narrator understood why the poncho was needed, so choice C would not make sense in this passage.

7. C: The sentence should have the same meaning as sentences 17 and 18, be clear, make sense, and use proper grammar. Answer choice C combines the ideas in sentences 17 and 18 without repeating information. It also correctly joins the independent clauses using a comma and coordinating conjunction. Options A and B are both grammatically incorrect. Option D has redundant phrasing by repeating "gift shop."

8. A: The article *a* shows that sentence 4 is referring to only one tank, so a singular noun is needed. *Tanks* is a plural noun, and *tank* is a singular noun. This means choice A is correct. The preposition *from* would not make sense in place of the preposition *with*, so choice B is incorrect. The word *and* in this sentence is not used to join clauses or form a list of more than two items. This means that no comma is needed between *water* and *and*. This makes choice C incorrect. *Keep* is a present tense verb, and *kept* is a past tense verb. Sentence 4 is in present tense, so *keep* is used correctly in sentence 4. This means choice D is incorrect.

9. A: *Terra* means something is related to earth, and *aqua* means something is related to water. The rest of the paragraph talks about water and aquariums, so *aquarium* is the right word to use in sentence 5. This makes choice A correct. The word *pets* is not spelled using a double consonant, so choice B is incorrect. The preposition *with* would not make sense in place of *of* in sentence 5, so choice C is incorrect. The word *and* in this sentence is not used to join clauses or form a list of more than two items. This means that no comma is needed before *and*, so choice D is incorrect.

10. B: The adjective *easier* is used when comparing two things. The adjective *easiest* is used when comparing more than two things. In sentence 7, the four types of aquarium fish listed in sentence 6 are being compared. This means that the word *easiest* should be used instead of the word *easier*. This makes choice B correct. *Freshwater* is a compound word, so it is spelled correctly. This means choice A is incorrect. The pronoun *their* is a possessive pronoun, and the pronoun *they* is a subjective pronoun. In sentence 7, the needs of tropical freshwater fish are mentioned. This means that the possessive pronoun *their* should be used, so choice C is incorrect. The verb *have* can be used with plural or singular nouns, but the verb *has* can only be used with singular nouns. The word *they* is referring to many fish, so it is plural. It should be used with the verb *have*, so choice D is incorrect.

11. C: The preposition *through* does not make sense in sentence 9. The sentence should say that the fish can adapt to living in different environments, so choice C is correct. The verb *are* is a present tense verb, and the verb *were* is a past tense verb. Sentence 7 is written in present tense, so choice A is incorrect. When adding a suffix to a word with a silent *e* at the end, the silent *e* is often removed. When *-ing* is added to *live*, the resulting word is spelled *living*. This means that choice B is incorrect. Sentence 8 says that fish can adapt to more than one environment. The plural noun *environments* is used correctly in sentence 8, so choice D is incorrect.

12. A: The word *famous* is not spelled using the vowel team *ay*. The word comes from the root word *fame*, which is spelled with a silent *e*, and the suffix *-ous*. When the suffix is added, the silent *e* is removed, so choice A is correct. *Is* is a singular verb, and *are* is a plural verb. Since the sentence is talking about one mission, a singular verb, such as *is*, should be used. This makes Choice B incorrect. *San Antonio de Valero* is a proper noun because it is the name of a place. It should be capitalized, so choice C is incorrect. The word *that's* means *that is*. The pronoun *that* is not the correct pronoun to use in place of *San Antonio de Valero*, so choice D is incorrect.

12. and: The first clause in the sentence says that the Alamo was a successful mission. The second clause says that it served many purposes. The second clause adds information that supports the first clause. This means that *and* is the correct choice. The conjunctions *but* and *yet* are used to show contradictions. Since the clauses do not contradict each other, these choices are both incorrect. The conjunction *or* does not make sense in this sentence, so it is incorrect.

14. D: There are no grammatical errors or spelling errors in sentence 5, so choice D is correct. *Were* is a plural verb, and *was* is a singular verb. Since the sentence is talking about multiple church services, *were* is the correct verb to use. This means choice A is incorrect. The services were held inside of the buildings, not on top of them, so choice B is incorrect. Seasons are not proper nouns, so *summer* does not need to be capitalized. This makes choice C incorrect.

15. D: The Texas Revolution is a historical event, so it is a proper noun that should be capitalized. This makes choice D correct. *Was* is a singular verb, and *were* is a plural verb. *It* is a singular pronoun, so it should be used with a singular verb. *Was* is used correctly in sentence 10, so choice A is incorrect. The article *a* shows that the Alamo was only used as one fortress. *Fortress* is singular, but *fortresses* is plural. Since the sentence is only talking about one fortress, a singular noun is needed. This means choice B is incorrect. The word *during* is not spelled using double consonants. It is spelled correctly in sentence 10, so choice C is incorrect.

16. C: In sentence 9, the narrator shares that his or her father gave a speech once. This detail does not help the reader understand the other events and details in the passage. Sentence 9 interrupts the story and is slightly off topic, so choice C is correct. Sentence 4 is important to the story because it shows how the narrator prepared to write the speech. Sentence 7 is important because it explains why the narrator chose to write the speech about Martin Luther King Jr. Sentence 15 is also important to the story because it tells the reader what happened after the narrator's speech. This sentence also helps the reader understand that the narrator is eager to hear the judges' decision. Sentences 4, 7, and 15 are all details that help the reader understand the story's events and the narrator's thoughts and feelings. This means that choices A, B, and D are incorrect.

17. D: The sentence should include the same information as sentences 2 and 3, be clear, make sense, and use proper grammar. Answer choice D combines sentences 2 and 3, does not repeat information, and correctly uses a comma and coordinating conjunction to join independent clauses. The other three options are not grammatically correct.

18. B: Paragraph 3 is about the night of the speech contest. A sentence added at the beginning of this sentence should be related to the narrator preparing to give the speech. Choice B is correct because it is about the narrator preparing for the contest. It also provides a transition between paragraphs 2 and 3, so it helps the reader understand the events better. Choice A is incorrect because it belongs in paragraph 2. It is not a good introductory sentence for paragraph 3. Choice C is incorrect because it also belongs in paragraph 2. In sentence 8, the narrator has finished the speech, so choice C should be added before sentence 8. Choice D is incorrect because it is off topic.

19. A: Choice A is correct because it is related to the information in sentence 15. It also gives more information about the narrator's thoughts and provides a transition between paragraphs 3 and 4. Choices B and D are incorrect because they add details that do not help the reader understand the story. These details may be distracting to the reader. Choice C is incorrect because it should be added before sentence 15, not after it.

20. C: The word *spoken* is not spelled using any double vowels or vowel teams, so choice C is correct. The article *a* used before *country's* shows that the sentence is only talking about one country. The word *country's* is the possessive form of the word *country*. The word *countries* is the plural form of the word *country*. In sentence 2, there is only one country, so choice A is incorrect. The word *language* is not used at the end of a clause or a prepositional phrase. There is no need for a comma after *language*, so choice B is incorrect. The preposition *in* means something is inside of, throughout, or within something else. The people mentioned in sentence 2 live within the country, so *in* is the correct preposition to use in this sentence. This means choice D is incorrect.

21. D: Languages are proper nouns, so the name of a language should be capitalized. English and French are languages, so they must be capitalized. This means choice D is correct. The verb *has*, by itself, is used in present tense. The verb *had* is used in past tense. Sentence 4 is in present tense, so it needs a present tense verb. This makes choice A incorrect. *Two* and *too* are homophones, so they have different meanings. The word *two* is a number, and the word *too* means *also*. Sentence 4 describes the number of official languages that Canada has, so the word *two* is the correct word to use in sentence 4. This means choice B is incorrect. Since Canada has more than one official language, the plural noun *languages* is used correctly in sentence 4. It should not be changed to the singular noun *language*, so choice C is incorrect.

22. D: Sentence 8 is referring to more than one French speaker. The sentence does not say that the speakers own or possess the French language. The word *speaker's* shows possession, but the word *speakers* is the plural version of *speaker*. *Speakers* is the correct word to use in sentence 8, so choice D is correct. The word *difference* is a singular noun, so it should be used with singular verb. *Is* is a singular verb, but *are* is a plural verb. *Is* is the correct verb to use with *difference* in sentence 8, so choice A is incorrect. There is no need to add a comma after *used*, so choice B is incorrect. French is a language, so it is a proper noun and should be capitalized. This makes choice C incorrect.

23. D: *Itself* is a pronoun that is used with singular nouns. *Themselves* is a pronoun that is used with plural nouns. Since *people* is a plural noun, a plural pronoun should be used with it. This means that choice D is correct. The article *a* shows that the sentence is only talking about one group. This means that the singular noun *groups* should be used in this sentence, so choice A is incorrect. The word *most* can be added in front of an adjective to make it a superlative adjective. Superlative adjectives are used to compare two or more things. Nothing is being compared in sentence 9, so choice B is incorrect. *Identify* is a plural verb, and *identifies* is a singular verb. Since *people* is a plural noun, it must be used with a plural verb, like *identify*. This means choice D is incorrect.

24. B: The word "disrupt" means to interrupt or disturb something, so "disturb" is the closest synonym.

25. A: Answer choice A removes the unnecessary words while keeping the meaning clear and concise. The other options either lack clarity, are not very concise, or are grammatically incorrect.

26. C: A compound sentence contains two independent clauses separated by a comma and a conjunction or a semicolon. The only answer choice that correctly has this is option C.

27. B: An expository text provides factual information in a clear, informative way. It does not tell a fictional narrative or story, and it does not argue a point. It also does not list a bunch of steps to be carried out.

28. A: Answer choice A removes the unnecessary words while keeping the meaning clear and concise. The other options either lack clarity, are not very concise, or are grammatically incorrect.

How to Overcome Test Anxiety

Just the thought of taking a test is enough to make most people a little nervous. A test is an important event that can have a long-term impact on your future, so it's important to take it seriously and it's natural to feel anxious about performing well. But just because anxiety is normal, that doesn't mean that it's helpful in test taking, or that you should simply accept it as part of your life. Anxiety can have a variety of effects. These effects can be mild, like making you feel slightly nervous, or severe, like blocking your ability to focus or remember even a simple detail.

If you experience test anxiety—whether severe or mild—it's important to know how to beat it. To discover this, first you need to understand what causes test anxiety.

Causes of Test Anxiety

While we often think of anxiety as an uncontrollable emotional state, it can actually be caused by simple, practical things. One of the most common causes of test anxiety is that a person does not feel adequately prepared for their test. This feeling can be the result of many different issues such as poor study habits or lack of organization, but the most common culprit is time management. Starting to study too late, failing to organize your study time to cover all of the material, or being distracted while you study will mean that you're not well prepared for the test. This may lead to cramming the night before, which will cause you to be physically and mentally exhausted for the test. Poor time management also contributes to feelings of stress, fear, and hopelessness as you realize you are not well prepared but don't know what to do about it.

Other times, test anxiety is not related to your preparation for the test but comes from unresolved fear. This may be a past failure on a test, or poor performance on tests in general. It may come from comparing yourself to others who seem to be performing better or from the stress of living up to expectations. Anxiety may be driven by fears of the future—how failure on this test would affect your educational and career goals. These fears are often completely irrational, but they can still negatively impact your test performance.

Elements of Test Anxiety

As mentioned earlier, test anxiety is considered to be an emotional state, but it has physical and mental components as well. Sometimes you may not even realize that you are suffering from test anxiety until you notice the physical symptoms. These can include trembling hands, rapid heartbeat, sweating, nausea, and tense muscles. Extreme anxiety may lead to fainting or vomiting. Obviously, any of these symptoms can have a negative impact on testing. It is important to recognize them as soon as they begin to occur so that you can address the problem before it damages your performance.

The mental components of test anxiety include trouble focusing and inability to remember learned information. During a test, your mind is on high alert, which can help you recall information and stay focused for an extended period of time. However, anxiety interferes with your mind's natural processes, causing you to blank out, even on the questions you know well. The strain of testing during anxiety makes it difficult to stay focused, especially on a test that may take several hours. Extreme anxiety can take a huge mental toll, making it difficult not only to recall test information but even to understand the test questions or pull your thoughts together.

Effects of Test Anxiety

Test anxiety is like a disease—if left untreated, it will get progressively worse. Anxiety leads to poor performance, and this reinforces the feelings of fear and failure, which in turn lead to poor performances on subsequent tests. It can grow from a mild nervousness to a crippling condition. If allowed to progress, test anxiety can have a big impact on your schooling, and consequently on your future.

Test anxiety can spread to other parts of your life. Anxiety on tests can become anxiety in any stressful situation, and blanking on a test can turn into panicking in a job situation. But fortunately, you don't have to let anxiety rule your testing and determine your grades. There are a number of relatively simple steps you can take to move past anxiety and function normally on a test and in the rest of life.

Physical Steps for Beating Test Anxiety

While test anxiety is a serious problem, the good news is that it can be overcome. It doesn't have to control your ability to think and remember information. While it may take time, you can begin taking steps today to beat anxiety.

Just as your first hint that you may be struggling with anxiety comes from the physical symptoms, the first step to treating it is also physical. Rest is crucial for having a clear, strong mind. If you are tired, it is much easier to give in to anxiety. But if you establish good sleep habits, your body and mind will be ready to perform optimally, without the strain of exhaustion. Additionally, sleeping well helps you to retain information better, so you're more likely to recall the answers when you see the test questions.

Getting good sleep means more than going to bed on time. It's important to allow your brain time to relax. Take study breaks from time to time so it doesn't get overworked, and don't study right before bed. Take time to rest your mind before trying to rest your body, or you may find it difficult to fall asleep.

Along with sleep, other aspects of physical health are important in preparing for a test. Good nutrition is vital for good brain function. Sugary foods and drinks may give a burst of energy but this burst is followed by a crash, both physically and emotionally. Instead, fuel your body with protein and vitamin-rich foods.

Also, drink plenty of water. Dehydration can lead to headaches and exhaustion, especially if your brain is already under stress from the rigors of the test. Particularly if your test is a long one, drink water during the breaks. And if possible, take an energy-boosting snack to eat between sections.

Along with sleep and diet, a third important part of physical health is exercise. Maintaining a steady workout schedule is helpful, but even taking 5-minute study breaks to walk can help get your blood pumping faster and clear your head. Exercise also releases endorphins, which contribute to a positive feeling and can help combat test anxiety.

When you nurture your physical health, you are also contributing to your mental health. If your body is healthy, your mind is much more likely to be healthy as well. So take time to rest, nourish your body with healthy food and water, and get moving as much as possible. Taking these physical steps will make you stronger and more able to take the mental steps necessary to overcome test anxiety.

Mental Steps for Beating Test Anxiety

Working on the mental side of test anxiety can be more challenging, but as with the physical side, there are clear steps you can take to overcome it. As mentioned earlier, test anxiety often stems from lack of preparation, so the obvious solution is to prepare for the test. Effective studying may be the most important weapon you have for beating test anxiety, but you can and should employ several other mental tools to combat fear.

First, boost your confidence by reminding yourself of past success—tests or projects that you aced. If you're putting as much effort into preparing for this test as you did for those, there's no reason you should expect to fail here. Work hard to prepare; then trust your preparation.

Second, surround yourself with encouraging people. It can be helpful to find a study group, but be sure that the people you're around will encourage a positive attitude. If you spend time with others who are anxious or cynical, this will only contribute to your own anxiety. Look for others who are motivated to study hard from a desire to succeed, not from a fear of failure.

Third, reward yourself. A test is physically and mentally tiring, even without anxiety, and it can be helpful to have something to look forward to. Plan an activity following the test, regardless of the outcome, such as going to a movie or getting ice cream.

When you are taking the test, if you find yourself beginning to feel anxious, remind yourself that you know the material. Visualize successfully completing the test. Then take a few deep, relaxing breaths and return to it. Work through the questions carefully but with confidence, knowing that you are capable of succeeding.

Developing a healthy mental approach to test taking will also aid in other areas of life. Test anxiety affects more than just the actual test—it can be damaging to your mental health and even contribute to depression. It's important to beat test anxiety before it becomes a problem for more than testing.

Study Strategy

Being prepared for the test is necessary to combat anxiety, but what does being prepared look like? You may study for hours on end and still not feel prepared. What you need is a strategy for test prep. The next few pages outline our recommended steps to help you plan out and conquer the challenge of preparation.

Step 1: Scope Out the Test

Learn everything you can about the format (multiple choice, essay, etc.) and what will be on the test. Gather any study materials, course outlines, or sample exams that may be available. Not only will this help you to prepare, but knowing what to expect can help to alleviate test anxiety.

Step 2: Map Out the Material

Look through the textbook or study guide and make note of how many chapters or sections it has. Then divide these over the time you have. For example, if a book has 15 chapters and you have five days to study, you need to cover three chapters each day. Even better, if you have the time, leave an extra day at the end for overall review after you have gone through the material in depth.

If time is limited, you may need to prioritize the material. Look through it and make note of which sections you think you already have a good grasp on, and which need review. While you are studying, skim quickly through the familiar sections and take more time on the challenging parts.

Write out your plan so you don't get lost as you go. Having a written plan also helps you feel more in control of the study, so anxiety is less likely to arise from feeling overwhelmed at the amount to cover.

Step 3: Gather Your Tools

Decide what study method works best for you. Do you prefer to highlight in the book as you study and then go back over the highlighted portions? Or do you type out notes of the important information? Or is it helpful to make flashcards that you can carry with you? Assemble the pens, index cards, highlighters, post-it notes, and any other materials you may need so you won't be distracted by getting up to find things while you study.

If you're having a hard time retaining the information or organizing your notes, experiment with different methods. For example, try color-coding by subject with colored pens, highlighters, or post-it notes. If you learn better by hearing, try recording yourself reading your notes so you can listen while in the car, working out, or simply sitting at your desk. Ask a friend to quiz you from your flashcards, or try teaching someone the material to solidify it in your mind.

Step 4: Create Your Environment

It's important to avoid distractions while you study. This includes both the obvious distractions like visitors and the subtle distractions like an uncomfortable chair (or a too-comfortable couch that makes you want to fall asleep). Set up the best study environment possible: good lighting and a comfortable work area. If background music helps you focus, you may want to turn it on, but otherwise keep the room quiet. If you are using a computer to take notes, be sure you don't have any other windows open, especially applications like social media, games, or anything else that could distract you. Silence your phone and turn off notifications. Be sure to keep water close by so you stay hydrated while you study (but avoid unhealthy drinks and snacks).

Also, take into account the best time of day to study. Are you freshest first thing in the morning? Try to set aside some time then to work through the material. Is your mind clearer in the afternoon or evening? Schedule your study session then. Another method is to study at the same time of day that you will take the test, so that your brain gets used to working on the material at that time and will be ready to focus at test time.

Step 5: Study!

Once you have done all the study preparation, it's time to settle into the actual studying. Sit down, take a few moments to settle your mind so you can focus, and begin to follow your study plan. Don't give in to distractions or let yourself procrastinate. This is your time to prepare so you'll be ready to fearlessly approach the test. Make the most of the time and stay focused.

Of course, you don't want to burn out. If you study too long you may find that you're not retaining the information very well. Take regular study breaks. For example, taking five minutes out of every hour to walk briskly, breathing deeply and swinging your arms, can help your mind stay fresh.

As you get to the end of each chapter or section, it's a good idea to do a quick review. Remind yourself of what you learned and work on any difficult parts. When you feel that you've mastered the material, move on to the next part. At the end of your study session, briefly skim through your notes again.

But while review is helpful, cramming last minute is NOT. If at all possible, work ahead so that you won't need to fit all your study into the last day. Cramming overloads your brain with more information than it can process and retain, and your tired mind may struggle to recall even previously learned information when it is overwhelmed with last-minute study. Also, the urgent nature of cramming and the stress placed on your brain contribute to anxiety. You'll be more likely to go to the test feeling unprepared and having trouble thinking clearly.

So don't cram, and don't stay up late before the test, even just to review your notes at a leisurely pace. Your brain needs rest more than it needs to go over the information again. In fact, plan to finish your studies by noon or early afternoon the day before the test. Give your brain the rest of the day to relax or focus on other things, and get a good night's sleep. Then you will be fresh for the test and better able to recall what you've studied.

Step 6: Take a Practice Test

Many courses offer sample tests, either online or in the study materials. This is an excellent resource to check whether you have mastered the material, as well as to prepare for the test format and environment.

Check the test format ahead of time: the number of questions, the type (multiple choice, free response, etc.), and the time limit. Then create a plan for working through them. For example, if you have 30 minutes to take a 60-question test, your limit is 30 seconds per question. Spend less time on the questions you know well so that you can take more time on the difficult ones.

If you have time to take several practice tests, take the first one open book, with no time limit. Work through the questions at your own pace and make sure you fully understand them. Gradually work up to taking a test under test conditions: sit at a desk with all study materials put away and set a timer. Pace yourself to make sure you finish the test with time to spare and go back to check your answers if you have time.

After each test, check your answers. On the questions you missed, be sure you understand why you missed them. Did you misread the question (tests can use tricky wording)? Did you forget the information? Or was it something you hadn't learned? Go back and study any shaky areas that the practice tests reveal.

Taking these tests not only helps with your grade, but also aids in combating test anxiety. If you're already used to the test conditions, you're less likely to worry about it, and working through tests until you're scoring well gives you a confidence boost. Go through the practice tests until you feel comfortable, and then you can go into the test knowing that you're ready for it.

Test Tips

On test day, you should be confident, knowing that you've prepared well and are ready to answer the questions. But aside from preparation, there are several test day strategies you can employ to maximize your performance.

First, as stated before, get a good night's sleep the night before the test (and for several nights before that, if possible). Go into the test with a fresh, alert mind rather than staying up late to study.

Try not to change too much about your normal routine on the day of the test. It's important to eat a nutritious breakfast, but if you normally don't eat breakfast at all, consider eating just a protein bar. If you're a coffee drinker, go ahead and have your normal coffee. Just make sure you time it so that the caffeine doesn't wear off right in the middle of your test. Avoid sugary beverages, and drink enough water to stay hydrated but not so much that you need a restroom break 10 minutes into the test. If your test isn't first thing in the morning, consider going for a walk or doing a light workout before the test to get your blood flowing.

Allow yourself enough time to get ready, and leave for the test with plenty of time to spare so you won't have the anxiety of scrambling to arrive in time. Another reason to be early is to select a good seat. It's helpful to sit away from doors and windows, which can be distracting. Find a good seat, get out your supplies, and settle your mind before the test begins.

When the test begins, start by going over the instructions carefully, even if you already know what to expect. Make sure you avoid any careless mistakes by following the directions.

Then begin working through the questions, pacing yourself as you've practiced. If you're not sure on an answer, don't spend too much time on it, and don't let it shake your confidence. Either skip it and come back later, or eliminate as many wrong answers as possible and guess among the remaining ones. Don't dwell on these questions as you continue—put them out of your mind and focus on what lies ahead.

Be sure to read all of the answer choices, even if you're sure the first one is the right answer. Sometimes you'll find a better one if you keep reading. But don't second-guess yourself if you do immediately know the answer. Your gut instinct is usually right. Don't let test anxiety rob you of the information you know.

If you have time at the end of the test (and if the test format allows), go back and review your answers. Be cautious about changing any, since your first instinct tends to be correct, but make sure you didn't misread any of the questions or accidentally mark the wrong answer choice. Look over any you skipped and make an educated guess.

At the end, leave the test feeling confident. You've done your best, so don't waste time worrying about your performance or wishing you could change anything. Instead, celebrate the successful completion of this test. And finally, use this test to learn how to deal with anxiety even better next time.

Review Video: Test Anxiety
Visit mometrix.com/academy and enter code: 100340

Important Qualification

Not all anxiety is created equal. If your test anxiety is causing major issues in your life beyond the classroom or testing center, or if you are experiencing troubling physical symptoms related to your anxiety, it may be a sign of a serious physiological or psychological condition. If this sounds like your situation, we strongly encourage you to seek professional help.

Online Resources

Due to our efforts to try to keep this book to a manageable length, we've created a link that will give you access to all of your online resources:

mometrix.com/resources719/terranextg4rl

It's Your Moment, Let's Celebrate It!

Share your story @mometrixtestpreparation